The Border Challenge

An Insider's View of Stopping Drugs at America's Borders

T. Michael Andrews

UNIVERSITY PRESS OF AMERICA,® INC.
Lanham • Boulder • New York • Toronto • Plymouth, UK

Copyright © 2012 by
University Press of America,® Inc.
4501 Forbes Boulevard
Suite 200
Lanham, Maryland 20706
UPA Acquisitions Department (301) 459-3366

Estover Road
Plymouth PL6 7PY
United Kingdom

Library of Congress Control Number: 2011936258
ISBN: 978-0-7618-5708-2 (paperback : alk. paper)
eISBN: 978-0-7618-5709-9

∞™ The paper used in this publication meets the minimum
requirements of American National Standard for Information
Sciences—Permanence of Paper for Printed Library Materials,
ANSI Z39.48-1992

Dedicated to two great fathers, Masonic brothers and lawyers:
Terrence "Terry" W. Andrews
and
Frank M. Moore

If we do not eliminate drugs, drugs will eliminate us.

—Hamid Karzai

Contents

Illustrations

Foreword

Prosecutors, be they state or federal, have a difficult job trying to convict an individual accused of committing a drug crime. Problems of proof may exist. Eyewitnesses may be reluctant to testify. The perception that drug crimes, especially marijuana smuggling, are "victimless" and therefore shouldn't be prosecuted can be hard to detect among members of a jury pool and harder to overcome. These problems intensify when the prosecutor's office must shift its priorities and redirect its resources from prosecuting an intractable array of drug crimes to any of the more sensational crimes of the moment—especially violent crimes with identifiable victims—like those depicted on a slew of TV shows featuring police and prosecutors' special victims units.

These difficulties are compounded exponentially when there is no consistent national policy on drug prosecution. The focus swings back and forth and round and round from treatment for offenders (after all, they just need help) to prison (it's not a victimless crime if they are stealing to support their habit) to interdiction (if we cut off drugs at their source, there won't be any drugs for consumers to use) to education (if users really knew how bad the drugs were, they wouldn't use them) and various shades of gray in between.

As a thirty-year prosecutor (retired) and former Supervisor of the Narcotics Unit of the Pima County Attorney's Office, I have experienced firsthand the frustration and confusion this lack of cohesive long-term planning has had particularly at the local level. Pima County, Arizona, which shares a 132-mile land border with Mexico that is extended an additional 120 miles through Indian Country, is probably the pre-eminent narcotics smuggling corridor in the entire United States. Across our international border, at ports of entry and at points in between, unprecedented levels of violence and victimization associated with drug crimes have been spilling over in recent years. We are in the cross-hairs of our nation's drug problem. Yet inconsistencies in federal policy combined with continually shifting resources make it hard, at a local level, to devise effective long-term strategies; to intelligently allocate funds and personnel; and, in general, to be able to plan beyond the short-term. Trying to understand why policies change, funds are re-allocated, grants are taken away and then, in a few years, all are given back is beyond the legal temperament of most line prosecutors, even those in management positions.

This book is an attempt to answer how and why decisions on national drug policy are made; and how those decisions play out on local law enforcement agencies and the offices of prosecutors whose job it is to sort out and implement those policies. Mike Andrews' career as a prosecutor in both the state and federal systems, and as an "inside the beltway" policymaker, gives him a unique perspective on this problem This book is a valuable resource for anyone trying to understand how our national drug policy came to be what it is and how, then, all of us can better work together to implement its goals.

Lou Spivak
Tucson, Arizona
May 2011

Preface

Like many Americans, I have often been intrigued by decision-making processes at the highest levels of our government in Washington, DC. Having served in the law enforcement field as both a state and federal prosecutor in Tucson, Arizona from 1997 to 2004, I have also been intrigued by the borders we share with neighboring states, particularly the legal boundaries that define national, state, or tribal jurisdictions. After prosecuting a number of narcotics and illegal drug cases in state and federal courts over this period, as well as certain felonies committed on Native American lands under the Major Crimes Act of 1885,[1] I learned all too well that drug traffickers respect no borders on drug trade but their own: Their dictates are alien to legitimately established governmental borders, institutional boundaries, legal limits and agency jurisdictions. As a prosecutor, I had been confronted with the extreme violence that drug traffickers perpetrate in order to push their products across geographical boundaries and legal borders into American communities as well as Indian Country.[2] I often had to weigh the destruction that addictive drugs, such as cocaine, heroin, and methamphetamine, bring to individuals, families and communities with the dangers faced by law enforcement personnel in the field. As a result, I came to understand the importance of protecting both our communities and our neighbors from illegal drug trafficking, and I felt compelled to challenge the existence of a complex and elusive subculture based on fear, intimidation and merciless greed, which operates in our midst.

When I first began prosecuting federal drug cases, I had assumed that America's drug policies, strategic plans and operations were made by men and women in windowless rooms, having meaningful discussions and ultimately making recommendations for senior managers to implement and to act upon. I also assumed that their decisions reflected benchmarks that were more familiar with the local scene and who thus provide the local intelligence relied upon to make the bulk of the drug arrests and seizures.

One of my loyal partners in law enforcement then suggested that I write a book explaining how drug policymakers at the federal level decide what action to take or not take when it comes to stopping drugs at our borders—a book that would explain how the priorities are determined; which agencies do what; and how the resources are allocated. He also pointed out that statistics on drug arrests and seizures are not enough to define success, let alone drive it. "When it comes to making drug arrests and seizures, policymakers need to understand how intelligence and enforcement come together, and what is needed to help us work smarter, stronger and faster," he urged.

His words rang in my ears as I sat at my desk back home, in Washington, DC.—It was often true that when drug busts occurred, arrests were made and the offenders were well prosecuted, the local, state and federal drug enforcement agencies had carefully coordinated their efforts across the legal and administrative borders that separate them. My partners in local law enforcement understood that turf wars among law enforcement agencies would only diminish our effectiveness in stopping drug traffickers.—But to write such a book, I mused, I would have to wait until the right time.

I begin with this personal story not only because it changed the focus of my career in law enforcement from that of a prosecutor and then policymaker to one of an educator, but also because the need to stop the rash of deadly drug violence within Mexico and across our Southwest border has grown more urgent along with the need to prevent illegal drug money from getting into the hands of insurgents. In the summer of 2008, I left my government post. It was then that I decided to take up the challenge of writing a book about the federal government's mission to stop the flow of illegal drugs coming across our borders—a mission that has evolved over the course of a century and expanded during a forty-year-long "war on drugs" to one that has been redirected in the decade since 9/11 to prevent the streams of drug money from financing drug cartels, insurgents and terrorists.

So with an aim to guide future drug policymakers and enforcement agents in the field, I set out to share my insights into several policy and program concerns, successes and missteps, based on my first-hand experience working inside the process of the drug war. To set the record straight, I feel compelled to discuss the lack of leadership at the highest level of our government and the gaps and disconnect between policymakers and enforcement operations in the field. For example, how can drug policymakers succeed with decisions based on turf war, power and politics, especially in the post 9/11 setting, while drug traffickers employ ever-changing methods to produce illegal drugs, stage their operations, smuggle drugs and money across borders, intimidate those who oppose them, and partner with terrorist organizations? Reflecting on these and other questions, my aim in writing this book is to better prepare students and working professionals who are dedicated to public service and law enforcement to work for our country's drug policy and enforcement agencies and to stop drug traffic at our borders.

T. Michael Andrews
University of Maryland, University College
Adelphi, Maryland
June 2011

Acknowledgments

This book would not have been possible without the strong support of my wife, Dr. Lisa Andrews; my mother Ann; my sister Michele; my nephew Matt; and my second family, Jim, Marie and Jimmy Tarsi, to whom I am thankful.

I am also grateful for the friendship, guidance and professional support I received from those individuals and organizations dedicated to protecting our children from the harm of illegal drugs: within the US Department of Homeland Security (DHS), Office of Counternarcotics Enforcement (CNE), former Directors Roger Mackin, Ret. Admiral Ralph Utley and my close personal friend Uttam Dhillon; Chief of Staff John Leech; Principle Assistant Director Scott Chronister; Executive Assistant Terry Daniel; and Assistant Director for Narco-terrorism Nate Phillips. Captain Patrick DeQuattro of the US Coast Guard, DHS, and Mark Wheat, former Staff Director, House Subcommittee on Drug Policy, Criminal Justice and Human Resources, provided guidance and constant support in ensuring that the DHS stayed focused on providing the necessary drug interdiction resources to the field. I also wish to give credit and pay respect to the many DHS agents not recognized here by name for their outstanding efforts in dangerous operations, including Special Agent Jaime Zapata of Immigration and Customs Enforcement (ICE), who was killed by drug traffickers in Mexico in February 2011.

I owe special thanks to my dear friends the Hon. Oliver Transue; Mike McCabe; Lou Spivak, former Prosecutor with the Pima Country Attorney's Office; Paul Banales, former Prosecutor and Pima County Superior Court Judge Pro-tem; Barton Fears; and Lawrence Seligman, former Chief of Police for the Pascua Yaqui Indian Nation. They, along with my great friends and colleagues at the University of Maryland University College and the District of Columbia and Maryland Crime Victims Resource Center, have provided trusted guidance and support over the years. Finally, I am thankful for the excellent editorial guidance and support of my editor in completing this book.

Introduction

Borders play an important role in controlling illegal drugs. Geographical and political borders mark the boundaries between sovereign states with their respective systems of government, law and economics, across which illegal drugs, money and weapons are traded. Our social policies serve as "fences," distinguishing legal and illegal uses of certain drugs, while legal and administrative limits define the roles of agencies within local, state and federal governments in controlling them. Communal borders can define "drug-free zones"—places that are off-limits to drug trafficking—as well as the conditions for acceptable uses of otherwise illegal drugs. Professional boundaries identify specific groups that, by virtue of their specialized knowledge and the public trust invested in them, can legally prescribe, administer, and market certain classes of drugs. In contrast, groups that trespass and conflict with the social norms and legal limits of society in order to make money from addiction to illegal drugs are considered drug traffickers. Among individuals, personal, psychological and spiritual boundaries may play a role in whether one follows a path to drug trafficking and drug-related crime or a path to drug addition and even recovery.

This book examines how the fronts on which the "war on drugs" was originally fought have become increasingly intertwined with security problems at our borders since 9/11. It considers why this war has become more expensive to fight, more difficult to stop, and more threatening to the safety and national security of the United States and the economic and political stability of countries in transition that are struggling to develop economically and politically and under the rule of law. Let us begin by considering the major targets of this war on drugs—then and now—and how the borders and fences that led to the way this war on drugs is currently being fought were put in place.

THE DOMAIN OF ILLEGAL DRUGS

The domain of illegal drugs in the United States was staked out nearly a century ago when the Harrison Narcotics Tax Act of 1914 restricted the sale of the morphine and, later, cocaine, making their nonmedical uses illegal. Derived from the opium poppy, morphine was then commercially available in medical remedies that could be obtained without a doctor's prescription, at least in the states that had not already enacted laws that limited its use for medical purposes. Under the Harrison Narcotics Tax Act, the legitimate medicinal uses of opiates and cocaine became controlled and taxed by the federal government; and reporting and recording systems were developed for narcotics dispensed by the medical profession.[1]

The boundaries of this domain were extended in 1919 to include beverage alcohol, when the National Prohibition Act prohibited its sale, manufacture and transport. Unlike opiates and cocaine, prohibition of alcohol was aimed not at controlling its "medicinal" uses—alcohol was widely prescribed for medicinal uses by the medical profession at the time—but the perceived evils of drunkenness and alcohol abuse, a moral and spiritual territory defined by temperance associations and pietistic religious denominations. More than a decade later in 1933, when the rise of a black market, organized crime syndicates, bootlegging, and increased crime rates were acknowledged to outweigh the moral and spiritual evils of drunkenness, and the cost of enforcement and the government's inability to generate tax revenues from the sale of alcohol became harder to justify, the National Prohibition Act was repealed as a failed social experiment. As a social policy, prohibition of alcohol did not succeed in reducing the supply of alcohol or the problems of its abuse.

The domain of illegal drugs was extended further in 1937 under the Marijuana Transfer Tax Act to include cannabis, commonly known as "marijuana," a Mexican slang term for cannabis. In a review of the history of drug legislation, Harrison, *et al.* note that during Prohibition, marijuana was considered a recreational drug and did not attract much attention in the news. Prior to the 1930s, "marijuana enjoyed an anonymity that minimized it being worthy of social policy or action. . . . Use of marijuana was limited to big city slums, minority groups (blacks in the South and Mexicans, many illegal aliens, in the Southwest, and jazz musicians); it had not as yet moved 'uptown.'"[2] But following the repeal of Prohibition, Harry Anslinger, the Federal Narcotics Commissioner, began a campaign against marijuana that reflected the mood of the times and was based in part on racial and anti-Mexican prejudices, using the popular press to raise fears among the public.[3] By 1937, all but two of the 48 states had passed anti-marijuana laws. As a national policy, the Marijuana Transfer Tax Act made it illegal to import marijuana, thus making marijuana the legal equivalent of narcotics from an enforcement standpoint.

By circumscribing the domain of illegal drugs, these early legislative attempts sought to reduce the supply of illegal drugs. Narcotics addiction declined in the United States by the early 1940s; but this decline in addiction is attributed to events of World War II, which disrupted the trafficking of opium from Asia through Europe.[4]

Following World War II, narcotics trafficking was thought to be a means of financing Communist party activities. As the new "superpower" in the world, the United States now had ideological and military interests in controlling the trafficking of narcotics from Asia during the Cold War.[5] Further legislative efforts aimed at reducing the supply of illegal drugs included legislation that stiffened the penalties for possession of opiates, cocaine and marijuana. The Boggs Act of 1951 established mandatory minimum federal sentences for possession; and the Narcotic Control Act of 1956 increased the penalties. This Act provided for death sentences for selling heroin to minors, as well as mandatory sentences of incarceration and no parole for second or subsequent drug violations. Forty years after the passage of the Harrison Narcotics Tax Act, the domain of illegal drugs included opiates, cocaine and marijuana; but after World War II, our concerns with trafficking extended beyond regulating their medicinal or recreational uses within our borders to broader political and ideological challenges.

THE DRUG CULTURE MEETS THE WAR ON DRUGS

In the early postwar period, drug use or "experimentation" was associated with the "Beat Generation," before eventually giving way to increased recreational drug use among educated, middle-class white society in the United States during the 1960s. During this era of social protest, social movements and social change, a confrontation between the "drug culture" and the "war on drugs" developed like a rising tide.

During the first wave, the "drug culture" emerged as a social phenomenon and became rooted in popular culture. Popular psychology explored the boundaries of the self and human consciousness, and experiments with psychedelic drugs, such as LSD (lysergic acid diethylamide), popularized by Dr. Timothy Leary, became a quasi-sophisticated way of exploring one's "self" and spirituality. Popular books by Carlos Castaneda depicting peyote rituals among the Yaqui Indians of the Southwest border region attempted to add an ancient and honorable cultural dimension to the spiritual mystique of psychoactive drugs. Popular psychology also influenced exploration within and among the arts of poetry, literature, painting, film and music. Psychedelic artwork decorated the covers of popular record albums, while the marijuana leaf—not the poppy—became a symbol of the youthful hippie counterculture.

During the late 1960s and early 1970s, the drug culture influenced styles and habits at a time of increased economic growth. Within the mainstream music industry, this led to promoting large-scale rock concerts that became cultural "happenings." The three-day Woodstock Music Festival in Bethel, New York, in August 1969, described by *Rolling Stone* as "the most famous event in rock history," was attended by 500,000 people and became an emblem of this genre.[6] Despite the peaceful celebratory ambiance of "Woodstock," the drug culture suffered two shocks in the fall of 1970 with the deaths of two of its icons—Jimi Hendrix and Janis Joplin—as a result of overdoses of sleeping pills and heroin, respectively. Their deaths cast a shadow over this cultural phenomenon, exposing its vulnerability.

The drug culture and the popular music culture were so closely identified with one another that President Richard M. Nixon accepted an offer by Elvis Presley to help communicate anti-drug messages to youth. A memorandum to President Nixon, dated December 21, 1970, written in preparation for a meeting that afternoon between the president of the United States and "the king of rock and roll," stated, "The problem is critical," and noted that teenagers suffered nearly 20 percent of the narcotic-related deaths in New York in 1970. The memorandum also pointed out that the deaths of Jimi Hendrix and Janis Joplin from drug-related causes "are a sharp reminder of how the rock music culture has been linked to the drug subculture."[7]

During the second wave, recognition of an association between drugs and crime moved drug issues onto the social policy agenda and shifted the focus of federal drug policies toward the aim of reducing the demand for drugs. Between 1960 and 1975, national crime rates increased steadily, before leveling off in the late 1970s. Violent crimes increased by an average of nine percent annually between 1960 and 1970. The national rate of violent crimes increased from 160.9 (per 100,000 inhabitants) in 1960 to 363.5 in 1970, reaching a rate of 487.8 (per 100,000 inhabitants) in 1975. Property crimes increased by an average of eight percent annually between 1960 and 1970. The national rate of property crimes increased from 1,726.3 (per 100,000 inhabitants) in 1960 to 3,632.0 in 1970, reaching a rate of 4,810.7 (per 100,000 inhabitants) in 1975.[8]

In August 1969, Dr. Robert DuPont observed a high rate of heroin use among the prison inmates in the District of Columbia. He advocated maintenance treatment with methadone, an inexpensive synthetic opiate that had recently been used experimentally with chronic heroin addicts at the federal narcotics rehabilitation and research facility in Lexington, Kentucky. The possibility of medical treatment for narcotic addictions offered not only a new approach to controlling drug abuse but also the hope of mitigating both drug abuse and crime by reducing the demand for illegal drugs.

In addition to this "crime epidemic," a bipartisan Congressional report in May 1971 described a "heroin epidemic" among US military personal returning from Vietnam. In the midst of growing opposition to the Vietnam War, recognition of drug use within the military presented a compelling reason to consider new strategies for controlling the demand for illegal drugs, and the US military responded by initiating a drug-testing program for returning service personnel in September 1971.[9]

With heroin at the top of the list of dangerous illegal drugs infiltrating military ranks, and marijuana—which was considered to be a "gateway" drug to heroin or cocaine, particularly among younger users—spreading in popularity especially among younger first-time users of drugs, drug treatment by methadone maintenance or other medical approaches became an acceptable strategy to control drug abuse and curtail the demand for illegal drugs. Reducing demand for drugs was also more pragmatic than prohibition, and enabled politicians to be "tough on drugs" while being "tough on crime." Drug abuse was thus seen as a social problem that could be treated by the medical and public health systems, a view that squared scientific advances in medicine with individual rights and social responsibilites. Thus, on June 17, 1971, as President Nixon decried drug abuse as "public enemy number one in the United States," the greater part of the federal drug budget was directed toward drug treatment rather than law enforcement.[10] The National Institute on Drug Abuse (NIDA) was established in 1974 to advance efforts to treat and prevent drug abuse through a scientific understanding of addiction and became part of the National Institutes of Health in 1992.

No sooner had federal drug policies become focused on treating heroin addiction and preventing crime than the pendulum of drug policy began to swing in the direction of law enforcement, and illegal drug use soon became ensconced as a problem of the criminal justice system. During this third wave, the confrontation between the drug culture and the war on drugs became a test of federal drug policy—a test that challenged the existing federal policy toward marijuana and the innocence of the drug culture.

In October 1970, the Comprehensive Drug Abuse, Prevention and Control Act consolidated existing federal drug legislation and established the frameworks for regulating pharmaceuticals as well as illegal drugs. Under Title II, known as the "Controlled Substances Act," it classifies drugs for purposes of regulating their manufacture, possession and use. At the time the law was drafted, marijuana was classified along with heroin as a Schedule I drug having no medical utility, the highest potential for abuse, and a lack of accepted

Chapter One

Thresholds of Concern

Public concern over the tenets on which the war on drugs has been fought has reached new thresholds in the decade since 9/11. This concern has been informed by changing public perceptions of the risks associated with marijuana and other illegal drugs; by outrage over untenable levels of violence associated with drug trafficking across our Southwest border with Mexico; and by growing recognition of the global complexities of controlling drug trafficking in a world challenged by terrorists and insurgents. Increasingly, our approach to the war on drugs is being openly acknowledged as a failure;[1] and the tenets of our drug policies are being challenged domestically and internationally.

THE THRESHOLD OF PUBLIC OPINION

One indication that public concern with the way the drug war was been fought has reached a threshold of changing public opinion is the popular support to decriminalize the use of marijuana for medical purposes. In this context, the term *decriminalize* refers to repealing criminal penalties under law for consumers who possess a given drug as well as physicians who may prescribe it for their patients, while retaining penalties for trafficking the same drug. Although the term *legalize* has been used interchangeably with *decriminalize* in public opinion polls, these two terms have different connotations in the context of drug policy discussions.[2]

The term *legalization* is broader in scope than *decriminalization* and implies some level of deregulation without necessarily specifying how controls that currently apply to legally available drugs might also be used. First, legalization of a given drug may eliminate criminal penalties for trafficking as well as possession for personal use, and thus may entail reduction of public

1

expenditures for drug enforcement. It may also allow for taxation of the production and sale of a given drug, similar to alcohol and tobacco. Second, legalization may also bring about important social consequences, such as reduction of violent crimes associated with drug trafficking, improved access to treatment for drug addiction, and reduction of public health risks associated with sharing needles. Advocates for legalization often cite such social consequences, noting in particular the reduction of crime following the repeal of prohibition of alcohol in the 1933, while assuming the experience of that earlier era is relevant to the current situation. Finally, legalization of a given drug may be interpreted to imply a level of safety associated with the use of that drug, a meaning that may or may not be intended.[3] Keeping in mind the connotations of these two terms, the following discussion of public opinion refers to the more limited scope of decriminalization.

In November 2004, in a nationwide poll commissioned by the American Association for Retired Persons of adults age 45 and older, 72 percent of respondents supported the use of marijuana by adults for medical purposes if a physician recommended it, a view that did not differ by age. Thirty-three percent of respondents thought adults should be allowed to grow marijuana for medical purposes, a view favored by a greater proportion of men than women (40 percent versus 28 percent) and by younger adults (45 to 59 years of age) than older adults (60 to 70+ years).[4]

Five years later, according to a poll conducted for ABC News/Washington Post in January 2010, 81 percent of a random sample of adults thought doctors should "be allowed to prescribe marijuana for medical purposes to treat their patents," compared with 69 percent in 1997. The lowest levels of support for decriminalizing marijuana for medical purposes in 2010 were found among persons over age 69, with 69 percent in favor, and among conservatives, with 68 percent in favor. The same survey found that 46 percent of respondents in 2010 favored "legalizing the possession of small amounts of marijuana for personal use," compared with 22 percent in 1997.[5]

As popular support to decriminalize the use of marijuana for medical purposes has grown nationwide, fourteen states have enacted laws that decriminalize the use, possession, or cultivation of marijuana for medical purposes as of January 2010. As shown in Table 1.1, at least nine of these states enacted laws after voters passed ballot measures, propositions or other initiatives in favor of decriminalizing marijuana for medical purposes. Most, but not all, of the state laws also decriminalize the cultivation of limited quantities of marijuana for medical purposes.[6]

In view of this trend, US public health officials reported an increase in marijuana use (for non-medical purposes) among teenagers since 2006, and a decrease in the percentage of teenagers who saw a "great risk" in occasionally

Table 1.1. States with Laws that Decriminalize the Use, Possession or Cultivation of Marijuana for Medical Purposes as of January 2010

State	Voter Support[1] and Year[2]	Medical Use[3]	Limited Cultivation for Medical Use
Alaska	Yes, 1998	Yes	Yes
California	Yes, 1996	Yes	Yes
Colorado	Yes, 2000	Yes	Yes
Hawaii	No, 2000	Yes	Yes
Maine	Yes, 1999	Yes	Yes
Michigan	Yes, 2008	Yes	Yes
Montana	Yes, 2004	Yes	Yes
Nevada	Yes, 2000	Yes	Yes
New Jersey	No, 2010	Yes (rules pending)	No
New Mexico	No, 2007	Yes	Yes
Oregon	Yes, 1998	Yes	Yes
Rhode Island	No, 2006	Yes	Yes
Vermont	No, 2004	Yes	Yes
Washington	Yes, 1998	Yes	Yes

Source: Data adapted from National Organization for the Reform of Marijuana Laws, "Active State Medical Marijuana Programs," http://norml.org/index.cfm?Group _ID=8088 (accessed March 21, 2010).

Notes:

1. Voter Support refers to statewide ballot measures, propositions, initiatives, questions or proposals in favor of decriminalization by a majority of registered voters in a given state.

2. Year refers to the year voters approved a measure or, in states without a voter measure, the year the state legislature first enacted a law.

3. The authorized medical conditions and amounts permitted for use, possession or cultivation vary from state to state.

smoking marijuana since 2004. The reported use of marijuana by teenagers had declined from 1997 to 2006, and researchers attributed the reversal of this trend in behavior among teenagers to their changing perceptions of the risks. They also linked the recent increase in the rate of adolescents who reported smoking marijuana to "the national debate over medical use of marijuana [which] can make the drug's use seem safer to teenagers."[7]

At the same time that the perception of "great risk" in smoking marijuana among teenagers was declining, and the use of marijuana among teens increasing, the potency of marijuana bound for street use was increasing. In 2009, the National Drug Intelligence Center (NDIC) reported that the University of Mississippi Potency Monitoring Project, which has monitored the concentration of delta-9tetrahydrocannabinol (THC), the psychoactive substance in the cannabis plant, in over 60,000 samples since 1975, found that the average concentration of THC in marijuana samples has risen steadily since 1999, and more than doubled between 1985 and 2007. In samples obtained from eradicated plots in the United States, Canada and Mexico, as well as from seizures by drug enforcement agencies, average THC concentrations increased from less than 4 percent in 1985 to 8.77 percent in 2006. By 2007, they reached 9.64 percent, the highest level recorded up to that time.[8]

The NDIC attributes the increased potency of marijuana to changes in growing techniques used by drug traffickers in response to an increased demand for higher potency marijuana. Higher potency marijuana is also more profitable and can be grown indoors year-round, yielding four to six harvests per year compared with one to two harvests of outdoor cultivation, and with less risk of detection and eradication. According to the Los Angeles County Regional Criminal Information Clearinghouse, the wholesale price of higher potency marijuana in Los Angeles may be 3 to 8 times higher, ranging from $2,500 to $6,000 per pound compared to $750 per pound of mid-grade potency marijuana.[9] To counter these trends, the National Institute on Drug Abuse (NIDA), which sponsors the Potency Monitoring Project, continues to warn teenagers of marijuana's harmful effects on health in an attempt to prevent continued or increased use of drugs in this young cohort.[10]

The significance of state laws decriminalizing marijuana for medical purposes are threefold: First, they are having the effect of marking the boundaries of a territory within the domain of illegal drugs—a reservation limited to the use, possession or cultivation of marijuana for medical purposes, one that is relatively off-limits to drug traffickers. By re-claiming this territory from federal jurisdiction, the states are raising a border dispute over marijuana that must be resolved between the states and the federal government. Second, by raising the issue of acceptable versus unacceptable uses of marijuana and its regulation by the states versus the federal government, the states are challenging the basic tenets of enforcement versus treatment that have stood as the pillars of federal drug control policies since the early 1970s.

Third, state laws based upon permissible use blur the borders between medical and non-medical uses of controlled substances. This creates the need for more sophisticated regulatory mechanisms for effectively controlling illegal drugs, which raises issues about how such mechanisms should be constructed and by whom. Should individual use be controlled according to one's risk of abuse? How should the risks be defined—by age, sex, health status, genetics, criminal background or other factors? If these state laws work effectively, their future significance may lie in forcing the development of more adequate regulatory mechanisms for drugs that involve a medical and legal determination of risk.

How we should resolve the issue of acceptable versus unacceptable uses of marijuana and its regulation by the states and the federal government is still unclear. One sign of an emerging federal direction and shift in priorities relating to individual use of marijuana was the October 19, 2009 announcement by President Barack Obama of new guidelines for drug enforcement by the DoJ. These guidelines are intended to focus on prosecution of drug trafficking and money laundering rather than situations involving medical uses of marijuana allowed under some state laws.[11] Whether this shift in federal enforcement priorities is prudent and effective may depend, in part, on the ability of the states to regulate this medical use of marijuana. Whether states that regulate the use of marijuana for medical purposes can establish borders that drug traffickers and drug users will respect without the interference of federal enforcement may become a test of both state laws and federal enforcement guidelines.

Responding to the challenge of rethinking the priorities of federal drug policy, Gil Kerlikowske, the Director of ONDCP under the Obama administration and an experienced law enforcement officer, describes enforcement and treatment as twin "silos" of drug policy that have led to an "either/or" approach of incarceration versus treatment. Instead of working in opposition, he proposes that the criminal justice system should serve as "a funnel to treatment;"[12] and treatment should aim at breaking "the cycle of illicit drug use, crime and incarceration."[13] Departing from the longstanding rhetoric of war, he finds the analogy of a war on drugs has become a barrier to drug treatment: "We're not at war with people in this country."[14]

THE THRESHOLD OF VIOLENCE

A second indication that the tenets on which the drug war has been fought have reached an unacceptable threshold of violence stems from the rise of murders, rapes, and kidnappings in Mexico, a high proportion of which are attributed to drug cartels, and the shocking level of violence practiced by drug cartels on both sides of the US-Mexico border. In 2009, the death toll related to drug trafficking reached 6,500 people in Mexico, which is estimated to be nearly half the total number of murders in the country.[15] Although recent news reports have focused on the gruesome violence, intimidation and retaliation practiced by Mexican drug cartels operating on both sides of the US-Mexico border,[16] the war on drugs has been transformed from the ground up since 9/11. Drug traffickers have responded to heightened security measures at US border crossings that are aimed at fighting terrorism and illegal immigration by finding new ways to use technology and infrastructure to elude them. In response to the mounting pressures on our respective governments to curtail the illegal drug trade and its economic consequences, the US government has increased its aid and support to the Mexican government's efforts to apprehend drug traffickers under the Merida Initiative and to curtail illegal drug trade and money laundering, estimated to be $12 to $15 billion dollars per year in hard currency alone in 2008. Such estimates exclude the amounts exchanged by wire transfer.[17] Even if our joint efforts can curb the illegal trade and money laundering, how our local, state and federal governments can or should control the demand for illegal drugs and their cultivation or production within our borders remains unclear and open for debate.

Considering our recent experience in attempting to control the use of methamphetamine ("meth") in the United States by enactment of the Combat Methamphetamine Epidemic Act in 2005, we will also need to take into account the consequences of our policies on both sides of our borders with Mexico and Canada. In 2005, a federal ban on the sale of the over-the-counter drug pseudoephedrine, the active ingredient in methamphetamine, was effective in curtailing the production of meth by clandestine meth labs in the United States. But given the continued demand for meth and the inscrutable culture of drug traffickers, the US ban on exporting pseudoephedrine resulted in a lucrative business opportunity for La Familia Michoacána, one of the most violent Mexican drug cartels based in the western state of Michoacán, known as a meth-producing region of Mexico. Profiting from the US ban, La Familia obtains pseudoephedrine from Asia, produces the some of the purest meth in Mexico, smuggles in half the US supply—where meth has become more popular than cocaine—and sets up its distribution centers in houses in middle-class suburbs, while paying-off Mexican officials, threatening death to "anyone" who interferes, supporting the poor people of Michoacán, and claiming to be devout Christians who abstain from drugs and keep them away from Mexicans. It has taken a joint drug enforcement operation, known as Project Coronado, four years to arrest 300 suspected meth traffickers tied to La Familia in the United States and three times that many in Mexico.[18]

In April 2009, former President Fernando Enrique Cardoso of Brazil, a co-president of the Latin American Commission on Drugs and Democracy (LACDD), presented the findings and recommendations of the LACDD at a conference hosted by The Brookings Institution in Washington, DC. He summarized the threat of drugs and the level of concern in Latin American countries in the following terms:

> Two of the most critical problems facing democracy in our region, violence and corruption, are closely associated with drugs. . . . Drug-related crime and violence in countries like Columbia and Mexico or in favelas of Rio have reached a level that can no longer be tolerated. We are no longer talking about collateral damage or unintended consequences of the war on drugs, but of a major political and social threat to democracy and security.[19]

Citing the need for a "paradigm shift" in drug policies as they affect Latin American countries, President Cardoso stated, "It's impossible to try to curb the expansion of drug consumption and trafficking without having a global approach to the issue. . . . From the beginning we felt the urgency of opening new channels of dialogue with the U.S. given the key role played by this country in the framing of regional and global anti-drug policies."

The LACDD's recommendations call for a paradigm shift based on "reducing the demand for drugs in the main consumer countries." President Cardoso noted that, "If we manage to reduce consumption through preventive actions and treat consumption as a matter of public health, we may break the grip of organized crime—reduce the opportunities for violence and corruption." In the meantime, "Prohibitionist policies based on eradication, interdiction, and criminalization of consumption simply are not working."[20]

THE THRESHOLD OF GLOBAL COMPLEXITY

A third indication that the tenets on which the drug war has been fought have reached a dangerous threshold of global complexity comes from news reports on the war against terrorism. Afghanistan has long been the world's largest grower of opium poppies, which are used to produce heroin. Based on a report issued by the United Nations Office of Drugs and Crime (UNODC) in 2006, opium cultivation in Afghanistan reached a record-high level of about 6,100 metric tons in 2006, a level far above the 4,600 metric tons that had been cultivated in 1999 while the Taliban was the ruling the country. Within one year, from 2005 to 2006, the area cultivated increased by over fifty percent, from 260,000 acres to 400,000 acres. According to Antonio Maria Costa, the executive director of the UNODC, most of the increase has occurred in five southern provinces that have been marked by a rise in "cultivation and trafficking, insurgency and terrorism, crime and corruption." He explains that Taliban insurgents have "encouraged and profited from the drug trade, promising protection to growers if they expanded their opium operations" and by exacting "levies in return for protection of drug convoys passing through the border areas they control." After earlier programs by international aid donors to eradicate poppy crops led Afghan farmers to oppose the US-led mission in Afghanistan, the Taliban's strategy of encouraging poppy cultivation has given insurgents an economic and political weapon it can use to provoke a reaction by the government that would turn farmers against the government. Thus, Costa notes, there is "a very strong connection between the increase in the insurgency . . . and the increase in cultivation."[21]

In response to this new front in the war on terrorism, the DEA has been conducting what has been described as a "war within a war." Since 2005, it has expanded its operations to disrupt the networks used to supply and traffic opium from Afghanistan.[22] Thus, the problems of fighting drugs and fighting terrorism have become increasingly intertwined, and the political and economic stability of poorer nations such as Mexico and Afghanistan often hang in the balance.

Whether we use marijuana from cannabis grown in Mexico; cocaine from coca grown in Columbia, Peru, or Bolivia; or heroin from opium grown in Afghanistan or Myanmar—the supply of these drugs consumed in the United States comes largely from less developed countries. According to Keven Casas-Zamora, Senior Fellow at The Brookings Institution and a former vice president of Costa Rica, the demand for these drugs comes at the expense of human lives, the environment and civil institutions in these less developed countries:

> Drug cultivation and drug trafficking *are* development issues. The trade in narcotics preys on very basic institutional weaknesses, on the feebleness and corruptibility of law enforcement mechanisms and ultimately, on the inability of the state . . . to have an effective presence in their territory. Drug trafficking takes full advantage of these weaknesses and makes them worse, generating parallel powers that contest the state's monopoly of force.[23]

In the United States, the supply of drugs makes it difficult for our government to prevent drug use; costly to treat drug abuse; and expensive to penalize citizens for drug-related offenses. From the perspective of individuals who use marijuana for medical purposes, the supply of marijuana makes it hard to refuse and even harder to be denied its use by one's government. But from the global perspectives of leaders of Latin America and the UNODC, the demand for drugs corrupts not only institutions of less developed countries but also our values.

Thus, the supply versus demand framework of drug policies is not strictly economic but also entails a delicate balance between individual rights and social responsibilities. More than ever, the way we think about drug policies must be finely attuned to the global social, political and economic realities of drug trafficking and drug use in our time.

Part I

THE FEDERAL RESPONSE
TO FIGHTING DRUGS

Chapter Two

Organizing and
Financing Drug Enforcement

As the federal government ramped up efforts to stem the tide of drug abuse and crime in the 1970s under the Richard M. Nixon Administration, the DEA emerged as the primary federal agency involved in drug enforcement; that is, seizures and federal drug busts. The establishment of the DEA in July 1973 signaled a major shift in emphasis from treatment of drug abuse to an enforcement approach. The DEA was founded within the Department of Justice (DoJ) and consolidated agents from Bureau of Narcotics and Dangerous Drugs (BNDD), the US Customs Bureau, the Central Intelligence Agency (CIA) and Office of Drug Abuse Law Enforcement (ODALE). Consolidation of these enforcement agencies within the DoJ supported its emphasis on enforcement of drug laws by the criminal justice system. The DEA would also assist in the development of interdiction and eradication measures. The DEA's jurisdictions are domestic and international, while the US Customs Bureau, which was then within the Department of Treasury (DoTrs), enforced laws pertaining to the import and export of all goods at the borders.[1]

From the early 1970s to the early 1980s, the DEA, the US Customs Bureau and the US Coast Guard worked closely with source countries such as Mexico, Peru, and Colombia to eradicate poppies, coca and marijuana. In 1981, the United States and Colombia ratified a bilateral treaty allowing extradition of cocaine traffickers from Colombia to the United States, making it harder for Columbian drug lords to escape prosecution. The United States and Mexico also began spraying Agent Orange to eradicate poppy fields in Mexico. As drug traffickers stepped up their efforts, so did the United States. The federal government responded by using military aircraft to help law enforcement detect and monitor illegal shipments of drugs coming to the United States. Although the military has no arrest powers, it does have technical capabilities that are useful to law enforcement.[2]

FINANCING DRUG ENFORCEMENT

Since the founding of the DEA in July 1973, every subsequent presidential administration, regardless of its party affiliation, has pursued the war on drugs to a greater or lesser degree; and the federal government has spent an ever-increasing amount of money attempting to reduce drug trafficking across our borders and illegal drug use and drug abuse within our borders. Estimates of the cumulative amounts spent on drug enforcement, drug treatment, and prevention of drug use since 1975 may vary as a result of inconsistencies in how federal agencies have reported their expenditures for drug-related programs in the past, as well as changes in accounting methods introduced in FY 2004 that affect what is included in and excluded from federal line item drug control budgets. However, according to the *National Drug Control Strategy: FY 2011 Budget Summary*, reported by the Office of National Drug Control Policy (ONDCP) in 2010, the federal government has spent over $117 billion trying to fight both the supply and the demand for illegal drugs in the United States since FY 2002. Between FY 2002 and FY 2010, over $45 billion of this amount has been directed toward treatment and prevention of drug abuse, the primary components of demand reduction. An additional $72 billion has been directed toward enforcement, including domestic and international enforcement programs and interdiction, the components of supply reduction. In FY 2010 alone, approximately $5.3 billion was allocated for treatment and prevention of drug abuse; and $9.8 billion was allocated for enforcement and interdiction.[3]

Five federal, executive branch departments currently have major responsibilities for drug enforcement and interdiction. Table 2.1 lists the departments that have received the largest shares of federal tax dollars to stop the supply of illegal drugs from entering the United States and to prevent illegal drug money from leaving the United States between FY 2001 and FY 2010.

It is important to note that Table 2.1 does not include the ONDCP or two of the largest federal agencies involved in preventing, treating, or researching drug abuse or addictions: namely, the Department of Health and Human Services (HHS), which funds NIDA and the Substance Abuse and Mental Health Administration; and the Department of Veterans Affairs, which funds drug-related treatment services by the Veterans Health Administration. Although it is not listed among the agencies involved in drug control in Table 2.1, the HHS received the largest drug-related budget authority within the federal government in FY 2010—$4,142.8 million—while the Veterans Administration received $405.0 million, and the ONDCP received $428.0 million in FY 2010.[4] Additional agencies that have a role in preventing drug use or abuse include the Department of Education, which funds school programs aimed at

Table 2.1. Federal Agencies Receiving the Largest Budget Allocations for Controlling Illegal Drugs, FY 2001–2010[1]

	Budget Allocation[2] (in millions)		
US Agency:	FY 2001	FY 2005	FY 2010
Department of Defense	$1,150.3	$ 906.5	$1,598.8
Department of Homeland Security	$-----[3]	$2,631.55	$3,752.2
Department of Justice	$8,074.1[4]	$2,671.5	$3,220.1
Department of State	$ 289.8	$ 898.7	$1,235.9
Department of Treasury	$1,262.0	$-----[5]	$ 59.2

Sources: Data adapted from Office of National Drug Control Policy, *National Drug Control Strategy: FY 2003 Budget Summary* (Washington, DC: The White House, February 2002) table 3, 7; *FY 2005 Budget Summary* (March 2004) table 2, 7; *FY 2006 Budget Summary* (February 2005) table 2, 8; *FY 2011 Budget Summary* (2010) table 2, 16.

Notes:
1. Not included here are agencies whose missions are directed toward research, prevention or treatment of drug use and abuse, such as the National Institute on Drug Abuse within the Department of Health and Human Services.
2. These figures are for enacted budget authority and may not include supplemental appropriations.
3. The Department of Homeland Security was established in November 2002. Its final budget authority for FY 2003 was $2,040.0 million.
4. The apparent reduction in budget authority for the DoJ between FY 2001 and FY 2005 reflects a restructuring of the federal drug control budget proposed in FY 2003, which changed how certain drug-related budget items are measured and reported, rather than actual reductions in federal spending for drug-related activities. These changes, which were implemented in FY 2004, include how the costs of keeping drug offenders in prisons or correctional facilities are reported. Prior to FY 2004, these amounts were reported in the DoJ's budget for drug control and are reflected here in the DoJ's budget authority for FY 2001. Starting in FY 2004, budget authority for drug enforcement expenses by the federal Bureau of Prisons is reported separately from the DoJ's efforts to control drugs; so it is not included in the DoJ's FY 2005 and FY 2010 line item budgets for drug control. These separate costs—which are viewed as "consequences of drug use"—are significant. For example, in FY 2010, the Bureau of Prisons received $3,204.0 million, which is not reflected here. For a discussion of the proposed restructuring the federal drug control budget, see the *National Drug Control Strategy: FY 2003 Budget Summary.*
5. In FY 2005, funds for the Organized Crime and Drug Enforcement Task Force were included in the DoJ's budget for Interagency Crime and Drug Enforcement (ICDE); so the DoTrs's portion and the DHS's portion are not reflected here in the FY 2005 and FY 2010 budget authority for these two agencies. Their respective portions are included in separate accounts for the DoTrs and DHS budgets for FY 2010.

preventing drug use among youth; the Department of Transportation, which funds the National Highway Traffic Safety Administration's Impaired Driving Program; the Small Business Administration, which provides Drug-Free Workplace grants; and the Department of Labor, which funds Job Corps and other programs.

REORGANIZING DRUG ENFORCEMENT

In the order of government funding for drug enforcement and interdiction shown in Table 2.1, the Department of Homeland Security (DHS) currently receives the most tax money in support of reducing the drug supply from entering the United States, based in part on its mission, size and functions. DHS was established in November 2002 under the Homeland Security Act, and undertook a major reorganization of federal agencies with law enforcement functions or air, land or sea border control functions. Effective March 1, 2003, 22 agencies were transferred to and reorganized within the DHS, including the US Customs Service from the Department of Treasury (DoTrs); the Immigration and Naturalization Services from the DoJ; and the US Coast Guard (USCG) from the Department of Transportation (DoT).

Within DHS, the newly organized Customs and Border Protection (CBP) spends the majority of its drug money on interdiction, followed by the USCG. Between CBP and the USCG, both agencies within DHS are responsible for detecting and seizing illegal contraband headed to the United States. Contraband includes people, terrorists, drugs, counterfeit goods, and money, to name a few. CBP's goal is to interdict and disrupt the flow of narcotics and ill-gotten gains across our nation and to dismantle the related smuggling organizations.

Immigration and Customs Enforcement (ICE), also part of DHS, also has a large role to play in investigating narcotics, people and money smuggling cases. ICE's mission is to dismantle high level criminal enterprises in the United States and abroad.

The second executive department receiving the most federal dollars is the Department of Justice. Within the DoJ, the DEA investigates drug crimes both domestically and internationally. The DEA also assists state and local law enforcement agencies with task forces and training. Along with DEA, the Federal Bureau of Investigation (FBI) and Alcohol Tobacco and Firearms (ATF) also have roles supporting law enforcement in apprehending drug dealers. The United States Attorney's Office handles the high volume of drug cases, while the Bureau of Prisons spends the majority of its money on treatment for inmates housed in its correctional facilities, including screening and assessment, drug abuse education, non-residential drug abuse counseling reviews, residential drug abuse programs, and community untraditional drug abuse treatment. As noted in Table 2.1, Note 4, budget authority for the Bureau of Prisons is reported separately from the DoJ's drug control budget.

Next, the Department of Defense (DoD) receives the third most allotted funds. DoD is the single lead federal agency whose drug related mission is to detect and monitor aerial and maritime shipment of illegal drugs to the United States. DoD also analyzes and disseminates intelligence on drug activity and provides training for US and foreign drug enforcement agencies as well as foreign military forces with drug enforcement responsibilities.

Finally, the State Department Bureau of International Narcotics and Law Enforcement Affairs (State INL) spends the great bulk of its drug war resources on international programs. Its goal is to develop, implement and monitor international counternarcotics control strategies and foreign assistance programs, and to advance international cooperation in order to reduce the foreign production and trafficking of illicit coca, opium, marijuana and other illegal drugs.

This list of federal agencies is not exhaustive. It does not include the many resources that are used at the state and local levels. In fact, the majority of all drug seizures in the United States are made by local law enforcement, including city police departments, sheriffs and state highway patrol officers.[5] The share of state dollars committed to the drug war is incalculable compared with federal dollars. This may be one reason why domestic law enforcement expenditures are no longer calculated in the overall national drug control budgets. If they were, the amounts reported would skyrocket.

THE OFFICE OF NATIONAL DRUG CONTROL POLICY

One of the problems with having so many offices in the federal government directed at a common cause is direction and leadership. The scope of bureaucracy can be overwhelming. If one department wants to take a different policy direction from another, this could lead to an immediate bureaucratic tie-up and in some cases pushback among the many agencies.

In the mid-1980s—as Columbian drug cartels were wreaking violence and havoc and trafficking cocaine with impunity, and highly addictive crack cocaine was becoming available on the streets in the United States and at a lower cost than powder cocaine—there wasn't a single agency that was responsible for coordinating all drug control agencies to achieve drug policy goals. Instead, numerous drug enforcement agencies as well as the agencies involved in prevention and treatment of drug abuse operated independently of one another, with little coordination.

To solve this crucial problem, the US Congress established the Office of National Drug Control Policy (ONDCP), a cabinet-level component of the Executive Office of the President of the United States, under the Anti-Drug Abuse Act of November 1988. As the lead federal agency speaking for the president on drug policy, ONDCP's stated mission is to establish policies, priorities, and objectives to eradicate illicit drug use, manufacturing, and trafficking, drug-related crime and violence, and drug-related health consequences in the United States.[6] As initially enacted, the law entitled ONDCP to be in existence for only five years. Like most government agencies, ONDCP has been reauthorized by appropriations in all but one of the subsequent four-year cycles: 1994; 1998; and, most recently, 2006, which reauthorized ONDCP through FY 2010. Following 9/11, Congress appropriated funds but did not reauthorize ONDCP for the FY 2002 cycle. (ONDCP was awaiting authorization for the next cycle as this book went to press.)

The director of ONDCP evaluates, coordinates, and oversees the international and domestic anti-drug efforts of executive branch agencies and ensures that such efforts sustain and complement state and local anti-drug activities. The director advises the president regarding changes in the organization, management, budgeting, and personnel of federal agencies that carry out our government's anti-drug efforts as well as federal agency compliance with their obligations under the National Drug Control Strategy (NDCS), an annual report of the ONDCP required by Congress. This annual report carries a tremendous amount of weight: it tells the American taxpayer how the federal government is doing with regard to stopping the flow of drugs into the United States and how well we are treating those who are addicted.[7]

ONDCP has far more power and reach than any other federal drug control agency. First, ONDCP has enormous government resources to lead the war on drugs. Second, ONDCP has launched massive public advertising campaigns on television, radio and the internet. Third, ONDCP statistics are likely seen as more legitimate because they represent the official work of the White House, and reflect the authority of the president of the United States. Given the power and scope of ONDCP, one is compelled to ask how its leadership role and influence have evolved; how they may have changed since the events of September 11, 2001; and how well ONDCP measures up to the challenges of leading this major federal effort.

Chapter Three

Political Leadership for Drug Policy

ONDCP was established during the Ronald Reagan Administration and evolved from the bipartisan work of then Sen. Joseph Biden, II (D-DE), Sen. Thomas Foley (D-MA), Sen. Strom Thurmond (R-SC), and Sen. Robert Michel (R-IL). William Bennett, the first Director of ONDCP—or "drug czar"—was appointed by President George H. W. Bush after he took office in January 1989. To date there have been six drug czars: William Bennett (1989–1991) and Bob Martinez (1991–1993), appointed by President George H. W. Bush; Lee Brown (1993–1995) and Gen. Barry McCaffrey (1996–2001), appointed by President "Bill" Clinton; John P. Walters (2001–2009), appointed by President George W. Bush; and Gil Kerlikowske (2009–), appointed by President Barack H. Obama.

Given the importance of leadership and performance for stopping illegal drugs and money at our borders, as well as the ongoing reorganization and financing of drug enforcement efforts since 1973, we will examine ONDCP's role in the context of political leadership for drug policy. To understand how ONDCP's leadership role and influence have developed and have been influenced by the events of 9/11 and the campaign against terrorism, we will first review the gradual expansion of ONDCP's role as mandated by the US Congress. Next, we will examine political leadership for drug policy over the course of the four presidential administrations from ONDCP's inception to 2011. We will also trace ONDCP's National Drug Control Strategy (NDCS) from 1989–2009, under the administrations before and immediately after 9/11. Finally, we will review ONDCP's leadership and performance in the aftermath of 9/11 from the perspective of congressional oversight.

EXPANSION OF ONDCP'S ROLE: 1988–2006

The Anti-Drug Abuse Act of November 1988 established ONDCP. Initially, ONDCP was charged it to implement a national strategy and to certify federal drug control budgets. The Act also specified that the strategy must be comprehensive and research-based and that it must contain long-range goals and measurable objectives to reduce drug abuse, trafficking and their consequences.[1]

In 1994, the Act reauthorized and extended ONDCP's reach to assess budgets and resources related to the National Drug Control Strategy (NDCS), an annual report to Congress. It also established specific reporting requirements in the areas of drug use, availability of illegal drugs and treatment of drug abuse. These requirements were consistent with the emphasis on curtailing drug use and demand during the Reagan Administration, which initiated the "Just Say, 'No'" campaign, which aimed particularly at youth.

In 1997, ONDCP's powers were expanded to include federal grants to community coalitions in the United States. These coalitions were established to reduce substance abuse among adolescents and to strengthen collaboration among organizations and agencies in both private and public sectors, reflecting a continuing emphasis on reducing drug use and demand among youth.

In 1998, ONDCP's reauthorization expanded its responsibilities to include authority to oversee High Intensity Drug Trafficking Areas (HIDTAs), an initiative involving local enforcement; to give greater demand reduction responsibility to the Counter Drug Technology Assessment Center (CTAC); to increase reporting to Congress on drug control activities; to establish a parents advisory council on drug abuse; and to reorganize ONDCP to allow for more effective national leadership. ONDCP was also directed to conduct a national media campaign for the purpose of reducing and preventing drug abuse among young people in the United States, consistent with its founding ethos.[2] Thus, ONDCP's mission going forward reflected additional functions related to demand reduction as well as local enforcement and information.

Although ONDCP's roles and responsibilities had expanded by 1998, in the aftermath of 9/11, the US Congress empowered ONDCP to do even more in its 2006 reauthorization. In addition to making the director of ONDCP a cabinet-level official, it created at least eight additional reporting requirements to Congress; established the Interdiction Committee and the Interdiction Coordinator and the National Interdiction Command and Control Plan (NICCP); outlined specific deliverables to the NDCS; required assessment of law enforcement intelligence sharing; established funding levels for HIDTAs; and designated an Anti-Doping Agency. Thus, since 9/11, the US Congress redirected the emphases of ONDCP's strategies and functions to give even greater attention to enforcement functions, including intelligence and controlling the supply of illegal drugs.

POLITICAL LEADERSHIP

Regardless of who controls the White House, the goal of reducing the amount of illegal drugs entering the United States has remained consistent. Yet it is clear that ONDCP's role has shifted over the years. This leads us to consider the role and influence of political leadership in controlling drugs and money from crossing our borders.

The George H. W. Bush Administration: 1989–1993

During the presidency of G. H. W. Bush, the ONDCP evolved from being a small office within the White House to one that had some teeth for the rest of the federal government. The G. H. W. Bush Administration is to be credited for establishing the framework for targeting drug cartels, utilizing covert intelligence for stopping the shipment of drugs at their source, and protecting financial systems from money laundering.

During the G. H. W. Bush Administration, the military's role in drug control increased. The president charged the DoD with tactical control of detection and monitoring of drugs. As a result, the DoD received a generous portion of the federal drug control budget to perform this function. There was also a big push for more interdiction along the Southwest border and in the Caribbean.

Finally, the G. H. W. Bush Administration led the effort to seize drug money with the creation of the Financial Crimes Enforcement Network (FinCEN) within the DoTrs. FinCEN, as it is known, is charged with maximizing information sharing among law enforcement agencies and its partners in the regulatory and financial communities. The mission of FinCEN is to safeguard the financial system from the abuses of financial crimes, including terrorist financing, money laundering and other illicit activities. The FinCEN network approach encourages cost-effective and efficient measures to combat money laundering domestically and internationally. Since its inception, it has played a major role in assisting Mexico in its quest to stop drug money from infiltrating their banking system. Thus, looking back, the G. H. W. Bush Administration was at the forefront of seizing drugs and going after drug money.

Under the G. H. W. Bush Administration, the NDCS reports dating from 1989 to 1991 outlined significant details for cooperation and coordination between federal and state law enforcement agencies. For the first time, committees such as the Interdiction Committee and the United States Interdiction

Coordinator (USIC) were set up by ONDCP to discuss roles and responsibilities among the drug control agencies and the allocation of resources and sharing of information. The Interdiction Committee was made up of top principals of DoD, DEA, US Customs Bureau, the Immigration and Naturalization Service (INS), DoTrs and DoS. Also created were the Border Interdiction Committee (BIC) and the Public Land Drug Control Committee (PLDCC). Thus, for the first time, senior managers from these departments had White House leadership providing guidance through the chain of command.

The ONDCP's initial NDCS of 1989 emphasized interdiction and information systems: first, the development of a comprehensive information based approach to federal air, maritime, land and port of entry interdiction; next, enhanced computer support for interdiction through acceleration of machine readable documentation programs, such as installation of document matching readers at appropriate ports of entry and development of the international border interception system; and, finally, the expanded use of drug detection dogs, anti-vehicle barriers and container inspections and expanded secure communications systems. But it did not specify goals for stopping drugs from entering the United States or federal budget resources allocated to stopping drugs. As a strategy, it lacked the specifics needed to provide clear guidelines to the various drug control agencies for collaboration.

The 1990 NDCS emphasized interdiction by enhancing and expanding the role of the DoD in providing detection and monitoring of suspected drug traffickers. It discussed concentrated efforts on improved coordination of air, land and maritime interdiction to deter and intercept drug smuggling and illegal shipments of drug related money, munitions, and precursor chemicals. It also increased the focus on drug smuggling across the Southwest border of the United States. It also identified the Southwest border area as an "infected" area of concern. The NDCS also proposed that the federal government should establish a Border Interdiction Committee to facilitate interagency coordination of interdiction policy and programs. Finally, although this NDCS did not highlight statistical evidence of seizures, as in 1988 or 1989, it noted there was an increase in the THC (the psychoactive substance in the cannabis plant) content of marijuana between 1979 and 1988, and that the potency of THC doubled in ten years.

The 1991 NDCS emphasized for the first time that Border Interdiction and Security would be separated out for funding purposes. This was important because the White House wanted to draw attention to the need for providing the resources for protecting the border. For the first time, it also mentioned deployable assets that were being used to protect the border. These assets included Maritime Patrol Aircraft (MPA) and helicopters along the Southwest border and in the Bahamas and Puerto Rico and ground based aerostat radar as a force multiplier. The 1991 NDCS also reported statistics on seizures from 1988 to1990.

In addition, the 1991 NDCS emphasized that the use of drug detection dogs had proven to be a cost effective way to increase the efficiency of law enforcement efforts. This strategy dealt with attacking precursor and essential chemicals and laundered money. Accordingly, ONDCP found that better intelligence and analysis of trends was necessary to stay abreast of the changing criminal activities of the drug traffickers. It also presented a budget history that illustrated how much money the federal government had been spending on the drug war.

Finally, the 1991 NDCS discussed the need for additional resources for dealing with the Southwest border and, for the first time, engaging directly with Mexico to seek cooperation. It emphasized working closely with the government of Mexico to develop measurements to pursue drug supply and demand control as a mutually beneficial endeavor.

The 1992 NDCS focused on the supply networks. It described how the primary goal of interdiction is to deny the smuggler the use of the air, land and maritime routes. It emphasized that this could be done be establishing and maintaining an active patrol presence and by intercepting and seizing illicit drug shipments entering the United States. The 1992 NDCS also emphasized command and control—a term of art that exercises the authority and direction by a properly designated command for the accomplishment of a mission. It noted that this process was much needed to integrate counterdrug planning by fusing the USCG, Customs, DEA and DoS. For the first time, this strategy acknowledged that although many intelligence centers—DEA; El Paso Intelligence Center (EPIC); Customs Service Command; Control and Communication and Intelligence (C3I); and DoD's Joint Interagency Task Forces (JIATF)—served as models for improvement, there was a need to collect, streamline and improve the intelligence collection, analysis and dissemination of the tactical and operational levels.

The 1992 NDCS also estimated that over 75 percent of cocaine seized by US Customs and 70 percent of cocaine seized by the USCG involved the use of confidential informants. It reported that 1992 was a record year for seizures of heroin, hashish and cocaine because of the emphasis on restricting transshipment. Surprisingly, however, unlike 1991 NDCS, which emphasized the need to do a better job of interdicting drugs along the Southwest border, the 1992 NDCS did not mention the Southwest border or seizing money.

The "Bill" Clinton Administration: 1993–2001

The Bill Clinton Administration focused its early drug strategies on education and treatment. Initially, President Clinton did not emphasize his predecessor's commitment to interdiction or supply zone eradication and intelligence; but after struggling to find direction in drug policy from 1993 to 1994, the ONDCP's 1994 NDCS laid out aggressive goals for stopping the supply of and reducing the demand for drugs. The strategy also laid out methods of sharing information and using intelligence-based interdiction as a start. More importantly, one sees a total commitment by the federal government in terms of resources to help state, local, tribal and federal law enforcement.

From 1996 through 2000, the Clinton Administration changed directions and tactics and, for the first time, laid out goals for drug policy administration, which had not been done in the previous administration. In 1996, President Clinton, by executive order, charged ONDCP to produce outcome measures of effectiveness; that is, performance measures. The executive order designated the director of ONDCP as the chief spokesman for drug control within the federal government. It made the ONDCP more accountable to taxpayers because it laid out performance measures of success.

During the Clinton Administration, ONDCP had two strong leaders: Lee Brown a long-time law enforcement officer who had led police departments in Atlanta, Houston and New York; and Gen. Barry McCaffrey, who was a decorated combat veteran and the youngest general in the army at the time he retired. Both directors eventually pursued an aggressive approach to enforcement.

The 1994 NDCS focused on source countries and outlined a comprehensive set of goals to achieve outcomes. It emphasized drug specific approaches of stopping the production of drugs. It recognized that the production of cocaine is largely limited to three countries that have a long record of counternarcotics relations with the United States: Colombia, Peru and Ecuador. Because heroin and marijuana involve several drug-producing countries around the world, ONDCP outlined a strategy for dealing with each host country or region. The two biggest countries emphasized for support were Mexico and Colombia. Interestingly enough, funding for these countries had dropped. US drug assistance for Mexico went from $20 million in 1993 to $1 million in 1994. As a result, Colombia branched off from a cocaine-producing country to that of a heroin-producing country as well. This enabled greater competition in the heroin market in the United States. In response, ONDCP took leadership for developing a cocaine and heroin strategy to be implemented.

The 1994 NDCS also changed the way programs attacked the flow of drugs to essentially in all places, at all the times: that is, in the source countries; in the transit zone (a six million square mile area that encompasses Central America, Mexico, the Caribbean Sea, the Gulf of Mexico, and the Eastern Pacific Ocean); and along the US border and within US communities. The 1994 strategy focused on (1) assisting nations that demonstrate the will to address the problems of drug use and trafficking; (2) destroying domestic and international drug trafficking organizations; (3) exercising more selective and flexible interdiction programs; and (4) enhancing the quality of traditional investigation and prosecutorial activities while furthering new advances in policing. Also, for the first time, the 1994 NDCS did not emphasize statistical seizures as an indicator of overall progress, stating instead, "While measuring drug availability is not an unreasonable indicator of overall progress, it does not encompass the totality of our national efforts or reflect the true impact of law enforcement efforts on reducing crime."[3] Its goals included improving the efficiency of federal drug law enforcement capabilities, including interdiction and intelligence operations; strengthening international cooperation against narcotics production, trafficking and use; and supporting, implementing and leading more successful enforcement efforts to increase the costs and risks to narcotics producers and traffickers to reduce the supple of illicit drugs to the United States. Based on these goals, ONDCP would determine the level of success and/or improvements needed.

The 1994 strategy also produced two-year goals in which to achieve the following: reduce coca cultivation by 1996, by assisting and pressing Columbia, Bolivia and Peru to initiate or intensify crop control efforts through enforcement operations and economic incentives; stop the fast developing opium cultivation by 1996 through aggressive crop control programs in Columbia, Guatemala, and Mexico, by aggressively supporting crop control programs for poppy and coca in countries where there is a strong prospect for a record of success; and conduct flexible interdiction in the transit zone to ensure effective use of maritime and aerial interdiction capabilities. The strategy also named an Interdiction Coordinator to oversee these goals.

The 1995 NDCS followed the same vein as the 1994 strategy, emphasizing or supporting the goals that were discussed in the 1994 strategy; specifically, strengthening interdiction and international efforts. The 1995 report acknowledged that international drug trafficking continued to pose a direct threat in the United States and abroad. To support the goal of strengthening interdiction efforts, the 1995 NDCS emphasized the following: building strong intelligence capacities within the source countries; strengthening enforcement capacities in source countries so that major drug traffickers are targeted; fostering and building democratic institutions and strengthening law enforcement and judicial assistance. Also, the strategy emphasized using another tool to cripple funding for foreign nations by decertifying major drug producing countries from receiving State Department foreign aid. This would trigger a defunding mechanism for countries that did not deal with drug trafficking in their country.

The 1995 NDCS called for a twelve-month timeline for completing strengthened interdiction and international efforts. This action plan set in motion five targets to be completed: (1) coordinate the completion of a Presidential Decision Directive (PDD). This set in motion the genesis for the action plan of stopping cocaine and heroin from entering the United States. (2) work with federal drug control agencies to develop measures of effectiveness. (3) facilitate a ministerial conference to coordinate money laundering. (4) pursue congressional support for the PDD on cocaine and heroin. (5) expand international public diplomacy working with others to communicate the sincerity of the United States in counternarcotics activities and increase public support for counter drug programs. In doing so, both the 1994 and 1995 NDCS reports described clear objectives and timelines of accomplishment in fulfillment of the original directives of the ONDCP Act. This was important because it clearly described the, who, what, and when targets these objectives were supposed to meet.

The 1996 NDCS highlighted long-range objectives. The 1996 NDCS established measureable objectives in the area of education about the dangers of drugs; prevention advertising; strengthening law enforcement; improving the ability of HIDTAs to counter drug trafficking; promoting and providing treatment to drug abusers; reducing drug-related health problems including disease; conducting successful operations at the borders; improving law enforcement coordination; improving cooperation with Mexico; and deterring money laundering and using asset forfeiture to seize drug-related goods and money. In fact, one of the objectives in 1996 was to reduce drug use by fifty percent by 2007.

The 1997 NDCS re-emphasized two strategic areas: First, the Southwest border strategy indicated that the single geographic region that was plaguing the United States was the US-Mexico border. The report emphasized that the United States had countered with working groups such as the Southwest Border Initiative and the other operational task forces along the border to deter drug trafficking organizations. The other import area was the Caribbean back door. According to DEA estimates, this was the second most significant drug trafficking area, because cocaine sold in Puerto Rico was cheaper than anywhere else in the United States.

For the first time, methamphetamines were discussed as a possible threat. According to the report, "meth" was so easily manufactured and incredibly addictive that it was called the "poor man's cocaine." The 1997 NDCS emphasized that new production of meth was coming from Mexican drug trafficking organizations and not domestic sources.

An area that repeated existing strategies was the culmination of intelligence fusion centers. Here, the 1997 NDCS gently reminded law enforcement agencies to better coordinate actions so that operations and investigations were supported more effectively by information sharing. According to the

1997 NDCS, "We must have a system that can detect, monitor, and track domestic drug production and trafficking activities across a spectrum of illegal activities that includes cultivation, movement of precursors, smuggling and wholesale and retail distribution and laundering of profits."[4]

The 1998 NDCS emphasized a ten-year benchmark for reducing the amount of drug users, the amount of illegal narcotics coming into the United States, and the shipment of illicit drugs from the source zone should be cut within ten years. The NDCS noted that the aggressive goals of reducing usage and trafficking entailed years of critical assumptions. For example, it noted that to cut domestic cultivation of marijuana by fifty percent, there must be more readily available intelligence surveys to quantify such a target. The 1998 NDCS was the first strategy that incorporated the use of performance measures as a measure of success; in other words, the strategy outlined goals of achievement and gave target for achievement.

The 1998 strategy was also the first to report on coca cultivation in South America. From 1988 through 1997, Peru outpaced Colombia in cocaine production. In 1988, Peru grew 110,000 hectares of coca, followed by 120,000 hectares in 1992, and which was reduced to 65,000 in 1997 due to the herbicide spray campaign as well as continued eradication and regional air bridge interdiction campaigns against heroin producers in Colombia and Mexico. Finally, the 1998 strategy re-characterized interdiction efforts by renaming it the "Shield Air, Land and Sea Frontiers."

The 1999 NDCS focused on the decline of violence and drug related deaths while emphasizing that the social costs and taxpayers' burdens continued to climb along with the drug proceeds leaving the United States. In 1999, the NDCS designated certain law enforcement entities with tactical control over the border: that is, which agency is responsible for interdiction, investigation, and enforcement. For example, the US Customs Service (within DoTrs) had primary responsibility for ensuring that all movements of cargo and passengers through ports of entry (POE) complied with federal law. It was the lead agency for preventing and investigating drug trafficking though airports, seaports, land POE and all along the border. Customs was also responsible for stemming the flow of illegal drugs into the United States though the air.

The US Border Patrol was the primary federal drug interdiction agency focusing on drug smuggling between the POE. The USCG was the lead federal agency for maritime drug interdiction and shared that responsibility with the US Customs Service. The ONDCP emphasized that these agencies were the main federal response team at our borders. In addition to the agencies from the DoJ, DoTrs and the DoT, there were also twenty-three separate federal agencies and scores of state and local agencies involved in drug control efforts along the borders. To streamline functionality, DoJ, DoTrs, and DoT established the Border Coordination Initiative (BCI). This was organized as a five-year program and initially emphasized the Southwest border to improve effectiveness of joint efforts and to increase cooperation efforts supporting the interdiction of drugs, illegal aliens and other contraband from entering the United States. The ONDCP clearly recognized the problem of a lack of a coordinated effort to stem the flow of drugs from entering the United States and the 1999 NDCS marked the second attempt to coordinate law enforcement efforts at the border.

The 2000 NDCS report reiterated the 1999 strategy except that it separated out specific drugs instead of lumping all of the illegal drugs under supply reduction. For example, this strategy reviewed the use and seizure of five main drugs: cocaine; methamphetamines; heroin; ecstasy; and marijuana. According to the 2000 NDCS, the price and purity of cocaine showed a different pattern from the 1999 strategy: The price was down and purity of cocaine was up. Also alarming was the decline of the price of heroin, marijuana and methamphetamines (meth) and the increase in purity of THC in marijuana. Simply put, 2000 was a record year of cheap drugs. Besides the accessibility of cheap drugs in the United States, methamphetamine use and trafficking was starting to infiltrate traditional cocaine and other hard drug markets, making meth, in comparison, the "next crack epidemic." According to the 2000 NDCS, the number of individuals trying meth for the first time tripled in 2000, as did meth lab seizures by DEA. In 1995, there were only 327 lab seizures compared to 2,000 in 1999. As a result of increased drug use, drug-induced deaths increased by 1,500 from the prior year.

A main focus of the 2000 NDCS was on anti-money laundering initiatives. In light of national security concerns posed by money laundering, Congress had passed the Money Laundering and Financial Crimes Act of 1998, which called for the development of a five-year anti-money laundering strategy. The DoT and the DoJ responded by releasing the first National Money Laundering Strategy (NMLS). This document provided a comprehensive overview of federal efforts to combat the subversion of our monetary system from a safe haven for drug traffickers.

A consistent and important theme repeated in the 2000 NDCS was the separation of operations from the supply zone, transit zone and arrival zone. The key component in the 2000 NDCS was the merger of two Joint Interagency Task Forces (JIATF) and the enhancement of JTF-South (JTF-S) as the lead task force in land and sea interdiction operations. JTF-S would conduct counter illicit trafficking operations, intelligence fusion and multi-sensor correlation to detect, monitor, and handoff suspected illicit trafficking targets; it would promote security cooperation and coordinate country team and partner nation initiatives in order to defeat the flow of illicit traffic. JTF-South has proven to be a successful operation and has contributed to the record amounts of cocaine seized in the high seas in recent years. Finally, the 2000 NDCS acknowledged that there had been a shift in drug trafficking from the Caribbean corridor to the Mexican and Gulf of Mexico corridor.

The 2001 NDCS, which was the last under the Clinton Administration, highlighted a record year for USCG interdictions: a record 139,919 pounds of cocaine, up by more than 30,000 pounds from the prior year. Just as important was the targeted enforcement to stop precursor chemicals sent from Southeast Asia from reaching the United States after entering ports in Mexico. Other new developments for the 2001 strategy were the creation of the National Counterdrug Intelligence Coordination (CDICG) and the Counterdrug Intelligence Executive Secretariat (CDX). The CDICG was created under the umbrella of the GCIP (General Counterdrug Intelligence Plan) to promote coordination between the national centers with counterdrug responsibility and to resolve multi-jurisdictional issues.

Along with successful operations by DEA and US Customs Service, the 2001 NDCS highlighted another operation that had proven useful: a bilateral cooperative agreement with Mexico called Operation HALCON ("Falcon"), which combined joint intercept aircraft and pilots stationed in Mexico and the United States. In 2000, Operation HALCON was responsible for the seizure of 5,547 pounds of cocaine; 27 aircraft; two maritime vessels; and 18,944 pounds of marijuana.

To summarize, the 1998–2000 NDCS reports provided several points of focus: the development of long-term national drug strategies; implementation of a robust performance measurement system; commitment to a five-year national drug control program budget; greater demand reduction responsibility; and increased reporting to Congress on drug control activities. Overall, during the Clinton Administration, there was more consistency in achieving goals and funding to support long-range interdiction programs. On the other hand, the NDCS reports of 2000 and 2001 included objectives for educating and enabling America's youth to reject illegal drugs as well as tobacco and alcohol; increasing the safety of America's citizens by substantially reducing drug-related crime and violence; reducing health and social costs to the public of illegal drug use; shielding America's air, land, and sea frontiers from the drug threat; and breaking foreign and domestic drug sources of supply. Sadly enough, these objectives were either unachievable or ignored.

The George W. Bush Administration: 2001–2009

The George W. Bush Administration's drug policy was hampered by fighting two wars in the Middle East. This makes it difficult to compare the

G. W. Bush Administration's legacy on the war on drugs when significant drug control assets were being deployed in the Middle East to fight the Taliban, Al-Qaeda, and the other rogue terrorist organizations. Under the G. W. Bush Administration, the DHS was established, drug control agencies were reorganized, and the drug control budget grew. The national drug control budget increased significantly from $10 billion in FY 2002 to $13 billion in FY 2008, including a generous interdiction budget increase from $2.1 billion in FY 2003 to $3.24 billion in FY 2008.

During the G. W. Bush Administration, ONDCP made efforts to move successful state and local task forces, such as the High Intensity Drug Traffic Area (HIDTA) under the DoJ's Organized Crime Drug Enforcement Task Force (OCDETF), and to eliminate key grants to state and local law enforcement to combat drugs in their communities. Another change that brought forth consternation throughout the federal government was the decision to diminish DoD's role for detection and monitoring. During the eight years of the G. W. Bush Administration, the DoD made every effort to take the money from the Central Drug Transfer Account and spend the money overseas on Middle East operations, instead of using it domestically in the transit zone. For example, DoD Secretary Donald Rumsfeld withdrew seven Army Blackhawk helicopters and their crews in the Bahamas that were supporting a highly successful drug interdiction operation known as OPBAT: Operation Bahamas, Turks & Caicos.[5] Yet, at the same time, the G. W. Bush Administration had one of the best coordinated and well-written strategies to combat drug trafficking along the Southwest border. The National Southwest Counternarcotics Strategy, which was launched in the spring of 2006, was a blueprint on coordinating efforts to assist in securing borders at the ports of entry and between the ports; sharing intelligence; prosecution; and stopping the flow of money going south.

Finally, one of the biggest object lessons from the G. W. Bush Administration's war on drugs was it reluctance to set long-range goals and objectives for the federal government's role in stopping drugs from entering the United States, as well as its failure to set performance measures, as required by congressional mandate. The administration's main focus for eight years was stemming marijuana use among kids. This focus, albeit important, meant that ONDCP did not focus on emerging drug trends, such as methamphetamine or prescription drug abuse.

While the G. W. Bush Administration's policy towards drugs was complacent and not forward-thinking, to its credit, his administration's efforts are notable in the area of enforcement. It set record levels for cocaine seizures, including the largest seizure ever recorded, when the USCG seized 42,845 pounds of cocaine, with a street value of over $500 million dollars, from a Panamanian flagged vessel in March 2007.[6]

The 2002 NDCS fell short of laying out a comprehensive drug strategy. It stated goals to achieve but did not offer a report card from the five-year goal that was set forth in the 1998 NDCS. It was supposed to provide policy makers indicators on what is working and what was not. If goals were not met, then one has to understand why and why not. Instead, the 2002 NDCS set priorities that were similar to those of previous years: (1) stopping use before its starts; (2) healing America's drug users; and (3) disrupting the market. The 2002 NDCS was heavy on prior-year drug statistical information on use, such as number of emergency department visits, marijuana use by metro areas, percentage of adult males booked for use of opiates by location, and the amount of drugs seized by foreign countries in the last ten years. Noticeably missing was any seizure data from US law enforcement.

The 2003 NDCS continued to highlight the three national priorities of stopping use before it starts, healing America's drug users, and disrupting the market. Focusing on the third leg of the stool, disrupting the market, there was hardly any mention of the newly created DHS, only traditional drug mission agencies such as US Customs and Border Patrol. The 2003 NDCS, like the 2002 report, focused primarily on attacking the supply of cocaine, highlighting budget increases for the DoD, and expanding support for Colombia and the Department of State's Andean Counterdrug Initiative. Accordingly, little attention was paid to transit and arrival zone accomplishments, goals and improvements and, more alarming, intelligence sharing, fusion centers or cooperation. Moreover, unlike the 2002 NDCS, which was heavy on statistics, there were hardly any data on seizures or arrests for law enforcement officials to gauge.

Also alarming was the reduction of "drug control" agencies from prior years. In 2002, ONDCP listed 41 drug control agencies; in 2003, only 15 were deemed drug control agencies in its proposed budget FY 2004. ONDCP reasoned:

> The aim of this proposal is to distinguish between funding for drug control efforts and funding for the consequences of drug use. The new drug budget presentation might show annual drug control spending to be several billion dollars less than what is currently reported. This presentational change, while dramatically lowering the amount of funding attributed to the drug control budget, will not have a negative effect on federal drug control efforts. In fact, it will improve those efforts by focusing on managing programs genuinely directed at reducing drug use.[7]

Essentially, this means that those agencies not classified as drug control agencies would not be under the umbrella of ONDCP, and ONDCP would not have to certify their budgets. This re-classification alleviated oversight from the White House and, therefore, these agencies could spend drug control monies with freer autonomy.

The 2004 and 2005 NDCS reports focus on different methods on stopping drugs from coming into the United States. The 2004 NDCS can best be described as the DEA year in review. The DEA no doubt had an exceptional year in arrests and seizures, but so did other state, local and federal law enforcement agencies. The 2004 NDCS failed to take into account seizures in the transit zone or discuss operational successes along the Southwest border. Instead, it focused on disrupting the market with continued eradication in Colombia, without discussing intelligence, task forces or arrival zone accomplishments. Unfortunately, it lacked goals and benchmarks as well.

The 2004 NDCS did, however, discuss for the first time the Afghanistan poppy cultivation threat. According to UN estimates, illicit poppy cultivation and heroin production generated more than $2 billion of illicit income, a sum equivalent to between one-half and one-third of the nation's legitimate gross domestic product. The drug trade in Afghanistan fosters instability and supports criminals, terrorists, and militias. Historic high prices commanded by opium continue to inhibit the normal development of the Afghan economy by sidetracking the labor pool and diminishing the attractiveness of legal farming and legitimate economic activities.

The 2005 NDCS described a more complete picture of all of the drug control agencies working to stop drugs from entering the United States. First, it discussed stopping the supply of cocaine and heroin from Colombia and South America through eradication and providing support to these countries. Next, it discussed successes in targeting the transporters through better intelligence. For example, the United States and our allies seized or forced the jettison of 210 metric tons of cocaine headed through the transit zone to US consumers. Adding seizures in South America, Mexico, and elsewhere, the United States and our allies removed 401 metric tons of cocaine. Besides the removal in the transit zone, the 2005 NDCS also discussed the high rate of seizure of meth at the Southwest border; but it said little on how to dismantle the organizations across the border from making meth or how to apply pressure on the Mexican government to assist.

The 2006, 2007, and 2008 NDCS reports can best be described as yearbooks of accomplishments, especially in terms of disrupting the market. With close to 1,000 metric tons of cocaine confiscated or disrupted by law enforcement in 36 months, these three years will go down as the largest drug busts and seizures in US history. Unlike the 2005 report, the 2006, 2007, and 2008

NDCS reports reflect a mix of success across the federal agencies at four fronts: first, Colombia and the eradication efforts, including Plan Colombia; second, successes in the transit zone from 2006 through 2008, mainly by the USCG, which set record levels of cocaine interdictions; third, Afghanistan was employing new resources to stop the poppy production and deny opium drug lords their illegal proceeds; and fourth, the Southwest border, which was exploring new strategies such as the National Southwest Counternarcotics Strategy and Implementation Plan.

Although the 2006, 2007, and 2008 NDCS reports addressed successes for law enforcement, what has been lost is that they did not tell decision makers how to win or provide clear objectives for years to come. Do more seizures in the transit zone indicate that the bad guys are losing? Certainly not—unless we know that we have seized all the drugs that they are producing for that year. Reality tells us that we do not know this information. As a result, we don't really know how well the federal response is doing against this threat.

The 2009 NDCS, the last one under the G. W. Bush Administration, can be summed up with one word: complacent. With all the hope from President G. W. Bush's NDCS from 2006 through 2008, the 2009 NDCS issued just prior to the inauguration of President Barack H. Obama, did not provide an adequate assessment from the last four, five, six or eight years regarding policies, operations and strategy. This probably has more to do with the continued oversight from "Drug War Hawk" Congressman Mark Souder (R-IN), the House Subcommittee on Criminal Justice, Drug Policy, and Human Resources, and the Senate Drug Caucus led by Sen. Charles Grassley (R-IA). Both members of Congress had called for the resignation of ONDCP Director John Walters.

However, the 2009 NDCP also reported considerable gains in drug intelligence. Accordingly, the US government now has more actionable intelligence and resources to interdict or investigate trafficking and more drug fusion centers set up along the Southwest border. The main concern here is that if we have better intelligence and better coordination, then why is drug flow still unstoppable? I would argue that there is a lack of significant planning for contingencies. It took the US government ten years to provide enough actionable intelligence it needed to stop the drugs, only to find out that we did not have the resources available to meet this threat.

The Barack H. Obama Administration: 2009–

Under the Barack H. Obama Administration, the Director of ONDCP no longer has cabinet-level status. However, Drug Czar Gil Kerlikowske has attempted to reassess the priorities of federal drug policy and move toward more strategic use of resources for treatment and enforcement functions. The FY 2010 National Drug Control Budget increased funds for prevention and treatment of drug abuse, while the NDCS emphasized enforcement along the Southwest border and on Native American lands.

Particularly, with regard to marijuana, DoJ resources would be targeted toward traffickers and not marijuana users. In October 2009, President Obama announced new guidelines for drug enforcement by the DoJ that are intended to focus on prosecution of drug trafficking and money laundering rather than situations involving medical uses of marijuana allowed under some state and local laws.[8] More recently, however, the DoJ has issued warnings to states that it intends to prosecute drug trafficking organizations purporting to be legitimate entities under state laws that allow medical marijuana dispensaries.[9] Working within the criminal justice system, ONDCP Director Kerlikowske has also aimed to remove barriers to treatment among convicted drug offenders in order to break the cycle of illegal drug use, crime and incarceration, signaling a shift in policies in favor of treatment and enforcement that targets high priority offenders.[10]

Under the Obama Administration, the US Congress passed the Fair Sentencing Act in July 2010, which amends the 1986 Anti-Drug Abuse Act to reduce disparities in mandatory sentences for crack versus power cocaine offenses by reducing the sentencing ratio from 100 to 1 to about 18 to 1, and by eliminating the five-year mandatory minimum sentence for first-time offenders convicted of possession of crack. Reducing the sentencing ratios is expected to reduce racial disparities in sentences for cocaine offenses, refocus law enforcement resources on high-level traffickers, and restore a measure of confidence in the criminal justice system among the public.[11] Whether this amendment would be made retroactive to permit early release for drug offenders in federal prison was under consideration by the US Sentencing Commission in 2011.[12]

Border protection issues have also been at the forefront of the Obama Administration's drug control efforts as the information sharing lessons of 9/11 are being applied in connection with related issues of mutual interest. For example, in February 2011, President Obama met with Canadian Prime Minister Stephen Harper and agreed to increase border security and intelligence sharing among respective law enforcement agencies as part of a broader program to improve cooperation on trade and energy issues.[13]

Finally, in March 2011, President Obama met with Mexico's President Felipe Calderón and agreed to escalate intelligence-gathering in cooperation with the Mexican government and law enforcement agencies by using unarmed aerial surveillance over Mexican territory to locate and track drug traffickers. This controversial step has been viewed as an effort on the part the

US president to bridge a standoff with Mexico by responding to the "common threat" of transnational criminal activities that has been aggravated by illegal weapons and US demand for illegal drugs. At the same time, it is seen as a sign of pragmatism on the part of Mexico's president in balancing nationalistic sentiments, legal authority, social discontent, and threats of instability in agreeing to greater intervention by the United States.[14]

CONGRESSIONAL OVERSIGHT

Congress clearly authorized ONDCP to put in place a strategy that was dedicated to stopping the supply of drugs coming into the United States and to reduce the demand for them. These goals are still viable today, regardless of the shift in political administrations. Given that the United States is continuing to fighting the war on drugs, and if long-term objectives are unmanageable or are not being followed, then what kind of message is being sent to the drug control agencies that are supposed achieve them?

In an unusual step by Congress to address this issue, Congress issued a report entitled, *2006 Congressional Drug Control Budget and Policy Assessment: A Review of the 2007 National Drug Control Budget and the 2006 National Drug Control Strategy*, that exposed similar concerns based on a review of the 2006 NDCS and the FY 2007 National Drug Control Budget.[15] Specific examples highlighted in this report include congressional disapproval of ONDCP's leadership. According to the report, "The Committee has ongoing concerns that ONDCP Director John Walters has not been exercising the kind of active leadership, oversight, and coordination of executive branch drug control efforts envisioned by Congress when it authorized it in 1988."[16]

In addition, Congress was unhappy with the personnel chosen by ONDCP leadership to carry out direction. ONDCP Deputy Director for Supply Reduction nominee James O'Gara could not get confirmed by the US Senate. The Senate took the rare step of returning the nomination back to the administration, instead of simply not voting on the nominee.

The report goes on to note that ONDCP failed to take initiative in formulating an effective federal anti-methamphetamine strategy. ONDCP failed to effectively respond to the increasing pressure on federal law enforcement agencies to reduce drug enforcement in favor of homeland security and counterterrorism missions. Other concerns of Congress included the DHS's decision to reclassify drug interdiction as a Non-Homeland Security Mission within the DHS. This was of particular concern because DHS is a multi-mission agency, and reclassification of drug interdiction within DHS would gradually decrease resources for drug interdiction components by diverting resources to other non-drug missions.[17]

Another area of concern that Congress highlighted was the lack of planning for replacing aged DHS or DoD drug control assets, especially Maritime Patrol Aircraft (MPA). MPA are used for covering the transit zone and were instrumental in dismantling and disrupting over 254 metric tons of cocaine in 2005; 219 metric tons in 2004; and 176 metric tons in 2003.[18]

So, with the many responsibilities that ONDCP has acquired, do we still need an ONDCP as the catalyst behind the administration's efforts to curtail supply and demand for drugs, given this congressional oversight? ONDCP's current funding levels stayed around $26 million from FY 2004 to FY 2007. Is this money better spent at the departmental levels for coordinating both policy and operations? In each of the five major departments, there already exists a policy or operational component or both. Departments often have liaisons within their respective department to help coordinate and share information. Why draft a NDCS if its goals are ignored and separate drug control agencies draft their own strategies anyway? This seems duplicative and a waste of resources. Would the US government be better served by a smaller and more flexible drug office that is held accountable for monies spent and programs that do not work? Why add yet another layer of bureaucracy when the drug traffickers are nimble and can adapt to US resources being deployed?

One of the powers of ONDCP is to certify drug control budgets that are submitted to the president. In the last twenty years, there has only been one instance where the Director of the ONDCP exercised this duty by not certifying the drug control budget. This is like the Secretary of the Department of Agriculture telling the Department of Homeland Security they do not like the way DHS is screening plants coming into the United States. Both departments report to the President, right? The only way an office like ONDCP can function as an independent body is to reduce its size, stay on target with all goals set forth from previous drug control budgets, and have inspector general-like powers.—Remember the Inspector General (IG) does not report to the Secretary of their department and cannot be influenced politically.—This is the check and balance that the federal government needs.

Chapter Four

Turf Wars Empower Drug Traffickers

Ideally, agencies responsible for drug interdiction and enforcement should work together—seamlessly. But this is not always the case. Unfortunately, time and again, agencies want to receive credit more than cooperate. Agents may withhold information from another law enforcement agency in hopes that their home agency can ride in and look good for their department.

But aren't we all on the same team? What ever happened to the good guys versus bad guys? Working against the bad guys is hard enough, so why must I fight against teammates? Coach Lou Holtz summed it up best in *Winning All The Time*: "When you learn how to work with people, you can accomplish anything. To do this, you must subvert your ego in the service of a higher cause. You must never forget there is no I in the word Team."[1]

US CODE TITLE 21:
THE FEDERAL DRUG TRAFFICKING STATUTE

Inside the beltway, where ego drives policy and performance instead of sound reasoning, turf wars are all too common. A case in point involves drug investigations that have a nexus to the US border. United States Code Title 21 is the part of the US Federal Criminal Code that designates drug trafficking and selling drugs as a federal crime in the United States. Today, there are three federal law enforcement agencies with responsibility and authority to protect the US border: Customs and Border Protection (CBP), which has interdiction responsibility for all border related violations; Immigration and Customs Enforcement (ICE), which has the investigative responsibility for all border related violations; and USCG, which has maritime interdiction responsibility. The missions of these three agencies support and complement each other.

With regard to land investigations, CBP is authorized to interdict all aliens and contraband crossings along the US border. Similarly, ICE is authorized to investigate all such instances of border related violations, both inbound and outbound, with a notable exception: ICE currently lacks independent authority to investigate smuggling of drugs that cross the US border and end up within the United States.

The DEA has the authority to investigate all drug crimes both domestically and internationally. In order for ICE to pursue any investigation based upon a Title 21 crime—that is, drug trafficking—ICE is required to request approval by DEA. If DEA says "No" to the request, DEA systematically precludes ICE from doing its job. Hopefully, this should be the exception and not the rule with respect to drug violations.

RESPECTING THE CONTINUITY OF OPERATIONS

Drug trafficking organizations (DTO) respect no borders on drug trade but their own. When jurisdictional boundaries create barriers that inhibit cohesive and cooperative law enforcement efforts, they provide a haven for smuggling organizations and problems for law enforcement agencies. Investigations of transnational smuggling organizations are most effective when the lead investigative agency maintains the continuity of operations from start to finish. Transferring investigations between agencies after the transnational investigation develops leads within the United States is operationally unsound and could disrupt the continuity of drug smuggling investigations.

To be fair, DEA's position is that once any drugs crossover into the United States, they become domesticated. From its purview, the DEA has jurisdiction for follow-up investigation of those crimes. The DEA is one of the best law enforcement organizations in the United States, having tremendous institutional knowledge and the ability to go after international drug kingpins, utilizing intelligence and apprehending drug sellers. But with primary responsibility both domestically and internationally, doesn't it make more sense to allow federal law enforcement officers the authority to follow through and to make drug seizures away from the border?

With competition over limited resources, why would one agency stop another? For credit, access to funding or prestige? Much depends on how we measure agency performance and success. Statistics on seizures do not lend themselves to sharing information and working seamlessly if we can't see the big picture. On the other hand, the stakes are too high for turf battles to continue. We need to focus on the big picture.

INTEGRATING PERFORMANCE MEASURES

The Government Performance and Results Act of 1993 (GPRA) requires all federal agencies to develop performance measures to assess progress in achieving their legislative goals. The GPRA requires agencies to set multi-year strategic goals and corresponding annual goals in their performance plans to measure achievement of those goals and to report on their progress in their annual performance reports to Congress. These reports are intended to provide important information to agency mangers, policymakers and the public on what each agency accomplished with the taxpayers' dollars it has been allocated.[2]

When multiple agencies are involved in achieving a particular result, as with drug interdiction operations, the agencies need to coordinate the development of performance measures to ensure that they are complementary. Yet, in 2011, performance measures and approaches for assessing drug interdiction vary among core agencies and, in some cases, are not established by crucial drug control agencies.—Within the DHS, one notable exception is the USCG, which has measurable outcomes relating to reducing drug flow through the transit zone.—As a result, the success or failure rate regarding interdiction is problematic. In the FY 2011 fiscal situation, it is increasingly difficult to justify pouring millions of dollars into resources and operations if there aren't quantifiable measured outcomes. The lack of clear measureable goals makes it difficult to link policy determination with advocacy for financial resources from Congress if an agency cannot reasonably articulate outcomes.

More alarming is the fact that many agencies do not routinely track funds obligated to them by Congress. From FY 2000–2005, Congress allocated $16.2 billion to support counternarcotics and related programs in the source, transit and arrival zones.[3] Yet it is extremely difficult to track a pot of money when significant portions of this money may be used for other missions within an agency.

A case in point is the DHS Office of Counternarcotics Enforcement (CNE). When CNE was established in 2004, it was charged with developing performance measures for the counter-drug components of the DHS; providing an annual report to Congress describing the adequacy of resources within the DHS for stopping the entry of illegal drugs into the United States; and recommending the appropriate financial and personnel resources necessary for the DHS to fulfill this function. CNE's main purpose was to act as a mini inspector general to make sure the DHS did not depart from the traditional drug missions of the agencies that comprised DHS. ICE, CPB and USCG all have traditional drug interdiction missions, and Congress did not want all three agencies to focus solely on terrorism. The Director of the CNE was to coordinate efforts within the department to make sure ICE, CPB and USCG had clear objectives, coordinated efforts, sufficient budget and operational support to carry out their missions; and if any objective was lacking or diminished, to report back to Congress, through the annual report, for additional support.

In theory, this looked practical on its face, but why would DHS want another inspector general within its own department? The simple answer is that they wouldn't. Innocently enough, these previously established agencies that were now within DHS did not appreciate oversight from a newcomer, namely, CNE. On the other hand, if CNE were provided inspector general powers, it could help evaluate policies and budgets to make sure that the taxpayer is getting the most out of the money that is spent in the war on drugs. Then again, it would also seem to duplicate efforts.

As a result, taxpayers are often left in the dark as to what and where their tax dollars are going, despite assurances that the money is going to good use. But how does one determine good use when the government does not mandate targeted goals based on measured outcomes and require sound evidence of the results to show that the money is going to the stated purpose? Greater integration of strategic goals, performance measures and measurable outcomes among drug enforcement agencies with complementary functions would be a step toward achieving this oversight and mitigating turf wars

Part II

SECURING OUR BORDERS

Chapter Five

Fighting Drugs and Violence along Our Southwest Border

Harsh climate, vast geography, and sparsely populated areas of the American Southwest present unprecedented challenges to law enforcement and national security efforts along our nearly 2,000-mile border with Mexico. Between the thirty-three legitimate crossing points, the border between the United States and Mexico crosses hundreds of miles of open desert, rugged mountains, the Rio Grande River, and coastal waters that provide extensive isolated locations for cross-border criminal activity. Drug traffickers exploit the border in two directions, smuggling drugs from Mexico into the United States, and moving billions of dollars in illicit drug profits from the United States into Mexico. A majority of the illegal drugs consumed in the United States—cocaine, heroin, methamphetamine, and marijuana—originate from or pass through Mexico's land and sea territories, while huge illicit profits flow back to Mexican drug trafficking organizations (DTOs) across our common border. The DEA estimates that approximately ninety percent of the cocaine that enters the United States comes through Mexico; and according to a 2007 National Drug Intelligence Report, the majority of methamphetamine production is controlled by Mexican DTOs in both in the United States and Mexico.[1]

Drugs traffickers use various means of transportation—ranging from hidden compartments in cars and trucks; tunnels and aqueducts; backpackers on foot; lightweight aircraft and gliders; all terrain vehicles (ATVs); package delivery services; motorized launches; and rafts that are floated across the Rio Grande River—to transport drugs by land, air and water. The result is the flow of hundreds of tons of cocaine, methamphetamine, heroin, and marijuana from or through Mexico into the United States, of which only a small percentage is seized.

MEXICAN CARTELS

Drug trafficking organizations in Mexico have grown increasingly powerful, corrosive, and violent by exploiting vulnerabilities along the Southwest border to profit from lucrative illegal drug trade. Mexican cartels now dominate illicit drug distribution in the United States and control most of the cocaine flowing to US drug markets. Mexican kingpins exercise control over the drug trade in Mexican regions along our Southwest border and perpetrate alarming levels of violence as rival cartels contend with one another to expand territorial control.[2]

As depicted in Figure 5.1, four major DTOs control the flow of drugs across the Southwest border: the Tijuana Cartel, also known as the Arellano Felix Organization after its founder, Arellano Felix, controls areas along the west coast; the Osiel Cardenas Guillen Organization, known as the Gulf Cartel, controls areas along the Gulf Coast; the Federation Cartel controls areas in the central region; and the Juarez Cartel controls areas in Northern Mexico. In recent years, increasing competition and confrontations among these DTOs have led to unprecedented violence and intimidation, as these four cartels have wrought havoc within Mexico.

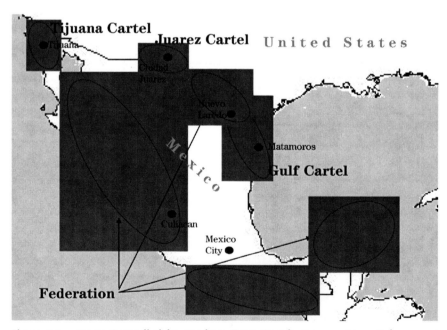

Figure 5.1. Areas Controlled by Mexican Drug Cartels. Source: Drug Enforcement Agency.

The Federation Cartel, operating in the State of Sinalo near the city of Culiacan, possibly has the most extensive geographic reach within Mexico. The influence of the Federation is so pervasive and intimidating that Mexican authorities have been reluctant to mount counternarcotics operations in the interior of that state.[3]

The Tijuana Cartel operates from the border city of Tijuana in the Mexican state of Baja California. Its activities are centered on the northwestern area of Mexico. According to local investigative journalists and US officials, this cartel exerts considerable influence over local law enforcement and munici-pal officials. The extent of corruption in Tijuana became evident in January 2007, when Mexican federal authorities forced local police to hand in their weapons in an effort to crack down on local corruption and drug-related violence.[4]

The Juarez Cartel is based in Ciudad Juarez, in the border State of Chihua-hua. According to DEA officials, the Juarez Cartel has extensive ties to state and local law enforcement officials. Over the years the Juarez Cartel has been implicated in a series of violent crimes linked to corruption, most notably the attempted murder of the governor of the State of Chihuahua by a former police officer in January 2001.[5]

Mexico's President, Felipe Calderón, declared Juarez the "tip of the spear" in the fight against drug cartels.[6] President Calderón sent 10,000 soldiers and federal agents into the city of 1.3 million to bolster the local police and to re-place corrupt or incompetent elements.[7] However, since the military marched in, violence related to the drug war has increased to well over 307 percent and has continued to rise, including violence against thirty Juarez police of-ficers who were hunted and gunned down in their homes.[8] As a result of this increased violence, some leaders inside Mexico have recommended raising the white flag and ceding control to the drug traffickers.

The Gulf Cartel operates out of the city of Matamoros on the Gulf of Mexico, in the Mexican State of Tamaulipas. According to DEA officials, the Gulf Cartel has infiltrated the law enforcement community throughout Tamaulipas, including the border port city of Nuevo Laredo, across the bor-der from Laredo, Texas. The situation has deteriorated so significantly that, in June 2007, when President Calderón sent federal army troops to stem drug-related violence and restore order in Nuevo Laredo, the troops were openly attacked by local police units, in a dramatic demonstration of the cartel's influence over local law enforcement authorities.

The Gulf Cartel has also spun off a criminal gang referred to as the "Zetas," which is primarily comprised of rogue former Mexican military commandos. Zetas are known for their carefully planned methods of violence and intimi-dation and are thought to be working closely with corrupt law enforcement officials.[9] Assassinations or kidnappings are planned and carried out so that no one is aware an attack has occurred until the victim's body is discovered the next day. In other cases, where police are alerted and give chase, it is common for Zeta's either to engage them in a firefight and win or to escape by tossing grenades at the police who are in pursuit. One particularly brutal method of killing is thought to be a signature of the Zetas: Zeta's are known to decapitate or mutilate bodies.[10]

DRUG VIOLENCE

Since 2007, drug violence and bloodshed in Mexico has been the subject of an increasing number of news stories and op-ed pieces, at least on the US side of the border. *Drug violence* frequently appeared in the headlines of articles dealing with Mexico in major newspapers, news magazines and on-line wire service reports, dating from 2008, such as these:

"Drug violence in Mexico: Can the army out-gun the drug lords?" *The Economist*, May 15, 2008;

Pamela Starr, "Mexico's spreading drug violence," *Los Angeles Times*, October 22, 2008;

Alfredo Corchado, "Mexico's drug violence expected to intensify in '09," *Dallas Morning News*, January 4, 2009;

Arthur Brice, "Drug War spins Mexico toward 'civil war'," CNN, February 18, 2009;

Sara Miller Llana, "Drug violence tarnishes Mexico's international image," *The Christian Science Monitor*, February 23, 2009;

George Grayson, "Mexico: Dealing with Drug Violence," *The Washington Post*, April 16, 2009;

Olga R. Rodríguez, Mark Walsh, Gustavo Ruiz and Natalia Parra, "Shootouts in Northern Mexico Kill 13 After Raid," *The Washington Times*, December 6, 2009.

In addition to *drug violence*, references to a *"drug war"* in Mexico appeared in headlines between March and June 2008, and some of these headlines conveyed *"fear"* or *"alarm"* on the part of US officials.[11]

Violence is the product of raw competition among cartels. When a top-level drug lord is killed or captured, an open battle ensues for control of the cartel's drug routes into the United States. The fact that the vast majority of killings occur among members of warring factions offers little consolation, especially when they occur in public places. Nevertheless, most law enforcement professionals understand that the increase in violence along the Southwest border is a sign that President Calderón's policies are working. President Calderón is the first Mexican President to take on the cartels since the arrival of the drug trade 30 years ago. His get-tough approach has already resulted in dismantling some of Mexico's largest criminal organizations. Given the magnitude of the cartels' threat to the Mexican government and public authorities, it is imperative that Mexican law enforcement not give up, despite the increased violence.

The threats in Mexico are also to be taken seriously in the United States. As a result of increased pressure applied by the United States, the cartels have reached the point of carrying out assassinations in the United States. Drug gangs in the United States target rich and poor alike, using intimidation and extortion, and have threatened and intimidated journalists covering Mexican drug traffickers. Reporters without Borders ranks Mexico as the most dangerous country for journalists after Iraq.

There is also evidence that Mexican cartels are also increasing their relationships with prison and street gangs in the United States in order to facilitate drug trafficking within the United Sates as well as wholesale and retail distribution of the drugs. Even more alarming, Mexican cartels are currently active in more than 230 US cities with branch offices dominating the wholesale distribution of drugs through the United States. With a presence in 48 of the 50 states, it is evident that Mexican cartels are the largest organized crime threat to the United States.[12]

The state of Arizona is considered the hub for Mexican cartels in the United States. It is estimated that 60 percent of all of the drugs that come into the United States from Mexico enter from the 370-mile border with Arizona. According to one report,"Phoenix is one of the main hubs for the Mexican cartels, which use the city as a distribution center. Thanks to the web of highways and interstates bisecting Phoenix, cartels have set up drop houses for marijuana, cocaine and meth in the city to be distributed across the country to dealers."[13] From Phoenix, the drugs are then distributed to other US cities where Mexican Cartels run their operations. For instance, authorities have confirmed the presence of the Sinaloa Cartel in at least 75 US cities; the Zetas in 37; the Juarez Cartel in 33; the Beltran-Leyva organization in 30; the Michoacán's family in 27; and the Tijuana Cartel in 21. These organizations are now operating now in every region of the United States and are expanding into new areas.[14]

The operations of the Mexican cartels in the United States are moving beyond the distribution of drugs. Because smuggling of drugs across the border has become more difficult and not always successful, cartels have decided to cultivate the drugs on the side of the border where it is going to be bought and consumed. It has been confirmed that these DTOs are growing millions of dollars worth of marijuana on US soil. Most of the marijuana fields that have been discovered are on public lands, including remote forests of National Parks, such as Mount Shasta National Forest and Sequoia National Park in California. One of the largest marijuana fields was in Sequoia National Park, where ten thousand marijuana plants with an estimated street value of $40 million were found.[15] In addition to California, authorities have declared that cartels are also growing marijuana in Kentucky, Tennessee, Michigan, Oklahoma, and Texas. In order to do so, the cartels hire illegal immigrants from Mexico who are sent to the distant locations with camping equipment and the appropriate irrigation tools to cultivate the plants and take care of them during the entire growing period, which can last up to five months. It is also necessary for the cartels to rely on people familiar with the area so the best spots for cultivation can be identified. The best spots must have plenty of water resources and must be close to roads for transportation but at the same time far enough away from local activity.

Although the illegal farmers can be arrested and the plants can be eradicated, Mexican cartels will not stop sending people to do this job because of the huge profits of the business. It is estimated that 60 percent of the cartels' revenue comes from marijuana sales. Undoubtedly, Mexican cartels are not willing to lose those earnings, which means they will keep finding new places in the United States to plant marijuana crops.[16]

Even though the illicit drug trade and the cartels' presence and operations from US territory are a tremendous problem, the violence associated with the Mexican drug cartels is a bigger concern. In the same way that drug cartels in Colombia used violence as a tool to react against the government's efforts to stop them, Mexican cartels have been doing the same to defend their illegal and profitable business. In testimony before the US Senate, Janet Napolitano, the Secretary of DHS, stated that about six thousand drug-related murders occurred in Mexico in 2008. That number represented double the number of casualties from the previous year, which had set a new record. About ten percent of those murders involved victims who were part of Mexico's military and law enforcement agencies.[17] Even though President Calderon, has been combating drug cartels since he took office in 2006, reports indicate that drug violence has continued to rise: According to a BBC report, "12,456 people were registered killed in drug-related violence in 2010 compared to 9,600 in 2009, bringing the total to 30,196 since President Calderon took office in December 2006."[18]

Owing to the proximity to US territory, violent battles are affecting US citizens. Although drug-related violent actions are not on the same scale as in

Mexico, some incidents on US soil suggest that the situation is getting worse. In recent years, cities across the United States have been experiencing more drug-related murders, extortion, and kidnappings. According to the DoS, the number of US citizens killed in Mexico increased from 35 in 2007 to 111 in 2010. Some of those Americans were working for Mexican cartels. However, others were innocent victims, including US law enforcement officers who were not involved in the business but unfortunately, were in the wrong place at the wrong time.

An increase in cross-border kidnappings in the Southwest states has also been observed. Members of cartels kidnap Americans on US territory and take them to Mexico, where they are held for ransom. On many occasions, even though the ransom demands are paid, the victims are tortured and then executed. In cities such as Phoenix and Tucson, Arizona, authorities report the highest number of kidnappings. In 2009, there were 370 kidnapping incidents in Phoenix and more than 200 in Tucson.[19] In response to this situation, authorities in these two cities created special police task forces to deal with this problem, which clearly was getting out of control.

THE TRIPLE THREAT

Since the events of September 11, 2001, the Southwest border region has assumed even greater significance to our national security, and drug smuggling along the Southwest border region has become a significant national security vulnerability that demands immediate action. Our Southwest border has become a nexus where three transnational threats converge: drug trafficking; alien smuggling; and terrorism.

Linkages between drug trafficking organizations operating in Mexico at or near the Southwest border, alien smuggling and, yes, terrorist groups are well documented. The US Border Patrol has reported that at times drug smugglers will arrange to send a shipment of drugs immediately behind vehicles containing illegal aliens, intending to divert US agents from efforts to interdict drugs. In addition, local officials have expressed concern over the risk that terrorists may utilize existing smuggling organizations' routes and methods to transport terrorists or weapons of terror across the border.[20] It has also been established that special interest aliens and terrorist groups have also tried to infiltrate the United States from the Southwest border.[21] In a 2007 briefing, John Michael "Mike" McConnell, the Director of National Intelligence, reported that Iraqi terrorists have been captured coming into the United States from Mexico. Our nation's top intelligence official expressed concern that terrorist groups such as al-Qaida, in the midst of regrouping and marshaling new recruits, are paying more attention to the Southwest border as they look for ways to enter the United States, where their goal is to cause "mass casualties." "Coming up through the Mexican border is a path," according to Mike McConnell.[22]

Terrorists could enter the United States or smuggle weapons of mass destruction (WMD) across the Southwest border by exploiting established routes and methods commonly used by drug smugglers and alien smugglers. If a criminal organization wants to bring WMD into the United States, more than likely they would use an existing drug trafficking route. Thus, the issue faced by federal, state, and local law enforcement agencies is how to close these gaps to drug traffickers as well as potential terrorist and illegal immigration traffic.

INTERDICTION AND INTELLIGENCE

This "triple threat" illustrates the importance of coordinating interdiction and intelligence. Effective law enforcement and interdiction along our Southwest border depend upon timely and accurate intelligence that provides not only tactical leads but also informs a common strategic picture. Since the early 1990s, when the Southwest border became the primary entryway for illicit narcotics into the United States, the national intelligence community and law enforcement agencies with responsibility for border enforcement have focused collection efforts along the border and within Mexico. Yet a comprehensive strategic picture of the drug threat at the border remains elusive.

Ongoing collection efforts along the border and within Mexico have been constrained by a number of factors. US law enforcement agencies at the federal, state, and local levels collect information that could fill many intelligence gaps, but information sharing remains insufficient, often due to jurisdictional responsibilities and the desire of law enforcement agencies to safeguard sensitive proprietary information. In many cases, law enforcement agencies lack the collection management systems, reporting officers, and trained intelligence specialists necessary to analyze and exploit existing data.[23] Tactical intelligence needs to be improved as well as the coordination of intelligence with the operational capability to respond.[24]

Drug traffickers often alter both the method and timing of their operations in response to border interdiction activities, so interdiction requires constant vigilance in checking people, equipment and commerce along the border as well a layered defense. Mobile and fixed checkpoints on US highways near the Southwest border play complementary roles in a layered defense against the triple threats of drug smuggling, illegal immigration, and terrorist activities. Through the use of internal checkpoints, persons who are not checked immediately at the border can be checked further down the line. In fiscal year 2004, 74 percent of the cocaine seized nationally by the US Border Patrol was seized at internal checkpoints.[25]

In addition to a layered defense on land, continued deployment of aerial surveillance is needed. Aerial surveillance includes cameras along border positions and unmanned aerial surveillance aircraft and drones, as depicted in Photo 5.1.

Despite tireless interdiction efforts along the Southwest border, massive amounts of drugs are still smuggled each year through legitimate crossing points. Criminal organizations, especially drug traffickers, have exploited the huge volume of passenger and commercial traffic that enters the United States via Mexican airports and maritime ports. Consequently, the vast majority of interdictions are the result of "cold hits"—which is enforcement jargon for drug detections that were not cued by prior intelligence. One of the most effective methods of detecting illegal drug trafficked through legitimate ports of entry (POE) is deployment of K-9 Units. According to one estimate, 60 percent of all drug seizures at POE result from canine detections.[26]

Photo 5.1.   Border cameras provide aerial surveillance of wide areas along our 2,000-mile land border with Mexico. Photo Credit: US Department of Homeland Security, Customs and Border Patrol.

To a large extent, major arrests and drug seizures are the result of close cooperation between US and Mexican law enforcement. When Javier Arellano-Felix of the violent Tijuana Cartel was captured, it required Mexican intelligence operatives working with US law enforcement to make it happen. When US and Mexico officials achieved the largest seizure of drug money in the Western Hemisphere—more than $200 million—it was due to cross-border law enforcement cooperation and coordination. Joint federal training initiatives have also led to bulk cash seizures at Benito Juarez International Airport, ranging from $1 million to $7.8 million.[27]

Mexico's main thrust against the cartels has been the deployment of its army, which is better armed and less vulnerable to corruption than are its police. However, the Mexican Army is relatively new to counternarcotics operations. To succeed against cartels, Mexico must continue to utilize and expand its technology at airports and maritime ports. Mexico must also enhance its resources dedicated to Southwest border investigations. Above all, Mexico cannot afford to retreat into appeasement.

THE MERIDA INITIATIVE

As Mexico and the United States attempt to fortify the 2,000-mile land border, as well as the maritime and air terminals that directly feed US ports of entry, the Mexican government's ability to confront its drug trafficking industry and its willingness to cooperate with US efforts directly affects our success in stopping drugs and money from crossing the border.[28]

US law enforcement officials are also aware that Mexican President Felipe Calderón's willingness to work with the United States on issues of security, crime and drugs is unprecedented. As a nation, Mexico is in the throws of an internal civil strife between the dual forces of corruption and drug trafficking and those of justice and the rule of law. It is a classic struggle of lawlessness against legitimacy. To win against the drug cartels, Mexico must be willing to continue the fight for the long haul, because this new brand of drug terrorists will not give up easily and is counting on defeating the will of the Mexican people. This cannot happen.

Since 2008, the US DoS has been supporting Mexico's counter-drug efforts through the Merida Initiative. This initiative is a security cooperation agreement among the United States and Mexico and the countries of Central America, with the aim of combating the threats of drug trafficking, transnational crime and money laundering. The assistance includes training, equipment and intelligence.

The joint initiative was announced on October 22, 2007, and in late June 2008, the US Congress passed legislation to authorize $1.6 billion for the three-year initiative. For the first year, 2008, the Merida Initiative provided $65 million to Central American countries and $400 million to Mexico ($100 million less than originally requested) for military and law enforcement training and equipment, as well as technical advice and training to strengthen the national justice systems. More than half of Mexico's share, about $204 million, was earmarked for the Mexican military for the purchase of eight used transport helicopters and two small surveillance aircraft. No weapons were included in the plan. Much of the funding will never leave the United States. It will go toward the purchase of eight Bell 412 helicopters, two small Cessna 208 airplanes, surveillance software, and other goods and services produced by private US defense contractors. While this request includes equipment and training, it does not involve any cash transfers or money to be provided directly to the government of Mexico or its private contractors. According to DoS officials, 59 percent of the proposed assistance will go to civil agencies responsible for law enforcement and 41 percent to operational costs for the Mexican Army and Navy. Although the initial cost for equipment and hardware that the military required is high, it is expected that future budget requests will focus increasingly on training and assistance to civil agencies.[29]

Chapter Six

Intercepting the
Business of Illegal Drugs

Drug trafficking is big business. Yet the public is often unaware of how drug trafficking organizations (DTOs) are set up and why they are in business. With the emphasis on stopping the supply of drugs coming into the United States, and despite media reports of seizures of multi-ton loads of cocaine and marijuana destined for US ports, the public is often unaware of the billions of dollars that flow freely across our borders to drug traffickers who produce and distribute even greater quantities of drugs than are seized. ONDCP estimates that Americans spend approximately $65 billion per year purchasing illegal drugs, and approximately $10 to $25 billion annually flows out of the United States as illegal proceeds from drug trafficking, either through money that is laundered or as bulk cash.[1] Even more alarming, less than $1 billion in illegal drug proceeds is seized per year. These amounts speak for how much more effort is needed to stop illegal proceeds from leaving the United States and getting into the hands of DTOs.

How do drug traffickers reap financial rewards? And what is their cost of doing business? Do US law enforcement agents have a better chance of stopping drug money from leaving the country than we do at stopping illegal drugs from entering? Applying the business model of a legitimate business in the United States to the balance sheets of DTOs, we would not find the profit and loss columns of doing business in a drug cartel or office. So, we cannot be sure just how much drug trafficking organizations spend and how many seized loads or seized money they can lose before going out of business. According to R. T. Naylor, Professor of Economics at McGill University and an expert in drug trafficking economics, "There is an endless supply of drug trafficking organizations and they will come in and take over when one office or cartel no longer can supply the money."[2]

DRUG TRAFFICKING ORGANIZATIONS

Why are drug traffickers in business? Simply put—to make money. According to the authors of *Drug Smugglers on Drug Smuggling Lessons from the Inside*, DTOs are set up in much the same way as legitimate businesses are in the United States. DTOs control the drug routes and regulate the drug flow into the United States by controlling access to areas along the border. Most DTOs start with the manufacturers, suppliers and brokers. Manufacturers are the part of a drug organization that grows the coca for cocaine, the poppies for heroin, or cannabis plants for marijuana. The suppliers include the chemists, the cooks, and the transporters of the chemicals or paste. The suppliers make the drugs and sell them to brokers. The brokers serve a number of strategic functions: they buy the drugs from the supplier; and they negotiate between the transporter and the distributor. Once agreements are made, the drugs are sent to an "office." Much like working at a business office in the United States, there is a team of about fifty to one hundred people in place to handle specific responsibilities. The office's job is to organize the details of a drug smuggling operation and to make the connections between the brokers and the transporters. There are a number of officers involved in a drug smuggling offense, each having primary tasks: supplying; packaging; transporting; distributing; and bringing back the money.[3]

For example, if a person wanted to send cocaine to the United States, he or she would have to buy the merchandise directly from the office. The office provides the merchandise to be transported. The office then turns over the merchandise for transportation. Generally, this is subcontracted out to various transporters. Transporters charge the office a fee and the people who assist in shipping charge a fee for using an airstrip or port.

The majority of drug traffickers are not in the supply chain but in the transportation mode. Transporters, as they are commonly referred to, are also the most likely to be arrested. Transportation managers work with the offices; but as soon as transportation arrangements are made, the responsibility rests solely on the managers to get the products to the United States. The transportation managers handle all of the responsibility ranging from resources, crew, logistics, transfer locations, and off-loads. Their costs add to the price of the drugs. For example, a transporter will usually charge the office $1,500 per kilo for cocaine. The transporter will then hire a transportation mechanism. If transported by boat, a boat captain is generally paid $250,000 to drive a boat from the Bahamas to Florida. An off-loader manager is paid $150,000 to unload up to 2,200 pounds of cocaine. If traveling by air, pilots may be paid about $3,000 per kilo because of the smaller amount of cargo room and the heightened risks of traveling by air.[4]

Typically, the transportation and networks used by Mexican DTOs to smuggle drugs into and throughout the United States are also used to return bulk criminal proceeds to the Southwest border (SWB) area. Typically, bulk currency is transported overland in shipments ranging from thousands to millions of dollars from major consolidation centers within the United States to staging areas along the SWB, such as Brownsville, El Paso, Hidalgo, and Laredo, Texas; San Diego, California; and Tucson, Arizona.

The main source of power for controlling money leaving the United States is the power over plazas. Plazas are simply the route one takes for transporting illegal goods into the United States. Having power over the plazas continues to be an important revenue stream for the cartels. Each route has a gatekeeper who imposes a tax on using the route. "Gatekeepers" collect "taxes" from smugglers on all illicit shipments, including drugs and illegal aliens, moved through these areas. The taxes are generally paid to the DTO that controls the area. The DTO then launders the proceeds. Gatekeepers sometimes resort to extortion, intimidation, and acts of violence to collect "taxes" from smugglers. Gatekeepers who control plazas can earn between $3 and $5 million per month in "taxes" charged to their DTO by moving drugs through the plaza. The cartel gatekeepers exercise a great degree of influence at entry points into the United States, to the point of having assassinations carried out on the US side of the border.[5]

However, one important money laundering technique used by Mexican DTOs is to use "money transmitters." This process involves wiring criminal proceeds, generally in amounts under $3,000 from distribution centers in the United States along the SWB. The wire transfers are cashed and consolidated, then smuggled in bulk form into Mexico by vehicle or people who walk across the border.

One of the checks and balances of DTOs is that the entire process is broken down into separate functional parts. Thus, if one functional part or group is infiltrated, the others may be protected. From a law enforcement perspective, this makes it more difficult to connect and trace not only the flow of drugs into the United States, but also the money paid for them that flows out of the United States.[6]

THE IMPORTANCE OF DRUG MONEY

Why is following drug money is important? According to a recent study, Mexico has emerged as a money laundering powerhouse.[7] According to a 2005 DEA study, in 2003 and 2004 there were, respectively, $9.2 billion and $10.2 billion excess US dollars present in Mexico that could not be accounted for from legitimate sources. DEA estimated that the four major drugs that are smuggled into the United States from Mexico—namely, methamphetamines, heroin, cocaine, and marijuana—generate as much as $22 billion per year for the sources of supply alone.[8]

Appearing before the Mexican Congress in October 2007, Mexico's Attorney General Eduardo Medina Mora reported that Mexican banks receive about $1 billion US dollars from legitimate US business annually, but they also receive up to $16 billion that does not have an explanation and which could be attributed to the flow of drug trafficking money.[9] Drug proceeds laundered in Mexico account for as much as four percent of the country's gross domestic product, or roughly $35.7 billion US dollars annually.[10]

Bulk currency smuggling is also gaining momentum as an alternative mechanism for the movement and placement of illicit funds. This alternative mechanism has emerged in response to the increasing effectiveness of regulations aimed at US financial institutions following the passage of the 2001 Patriot Act, including currency and suspicious transaction reporting requirements and "Know Your Customer" requirements in effect at most domestic financial institutions. The problem of bulk cash smuggling into Mexico was highlighted on March 15, 2007, when Mexican authorities announced a record seizure of approximately $207 million in US currency from the Mexico City home of pseudoephedrine broker Zhenli Ye Gon.[11]

Although currency seizures in Mexico have been increasing over the past several years, seizures should be considerably higher, considering the tremendous amount of illicit revenue flowing into that country. According to the 2007 International Narcotics Control Strategy Report (INCSR), the Mexican government seized $25 million in US currency in illicit drug proceeds in 2006.[12] However, a report issued by the National Drug Intelligence Center (NDIC) that same year estimated that out of $8.3 billion of illegal proceeds smuggled into Mexico, the Mexican government is seizing only 1.03 to 3.01 percent of the illicit proceeds entering the country annually, which amounts to only $24 million dollars annually.

FIGHTING DRUGS WITH FOREIGN AID

Mexican DTOs pose a direct threat not only to the Mexican state, but also to the security of the United States. Recognition of this threat led to the passage in 2008 of the Merida Initiative to combat drug trafficking in Mexico and other parts of Central America. The initiative initially provided $400 million to Mexico and $65 million for other countries in Central America, while the total aid package provides $1.4 billion to Mexico with an additional $2 billion in support for Central America, Haiti, and the Dominican Republic.[13]

Even with this new infusion of money, there are still gaps in Mexican financial institutions owing to archaic laws. For example, courier services present a quick and unregulated means of moving bulk cash within Mexico. Courier services such as United Parcel Service and Federal Express can transport large amounts of cash without knowing if the person sending the money has declared it. Alternatively, senders can use money transfer services such as Western Union where there is lax enforcement by Mexican law enforcement officials. As the United States cracks down on Mexican criminal organizations using traditional money laundering services such as *casa de combios*, DTOs will continue to use bulk cash smuggling as a method to return the profits back to the cartels.[14]

In addition, laws governing the purchase of real estate in Mexico make it easy for criminal organizations to invest and hold property that is not registered in their own names. Newly opened casinos and other gaming industries in Mexico are not currently subject to reporting requirements and are open to exploitation by criminal elements. Mexico lacks a single identification number for its citizens, and individuals can easily obtain fake identification, which makes it difficult for financial institutions to trace the activities of its customers.

PURSUING DRUG MONEY

Today, the US government relies on several agencies to go after drug traffickers' financial profits. Within the Department of Treasury (DoTrs), three agencies are involved: the Internal Revenue Service (IRS); the Office of Foreign Asset Control (OFAC); and the Financial Crimes Enforcement Network (FinCEN). Within the Department of Homeland Security, Immigration Customs and Enforcement (ICE) and Customs and Border Protection (CBP) are involved. Within the Department of Justice, the Drug Enforcement Administration (DEA) and the Federal Bureau of Investigation (FBI) are involved.

With the majority of these departments' budgets spent on apprehension, investigation and drug enforcement, relatively small percentages of their budgets are targeted to carry out money cases. The majority of border inspection resources are directed toward preventing drugs, terrorists or illegal immigrants from entering—not leaving—the United States. Problems of detection of southbound currency flows by law enforcement is also complicated by the high volume of cross-border traffic and by limited resources or emphasis on outbound inspection compared to inbound inspection, while the harsh terrain of the nearly 2,000-mile border with Mexico makes it relatively easy to move even large amounts of currency. In addition, each day, tens of thousands of individuals and vehicles cross land border points of entry and exit located in Arizona, California, New Mexico and Texas, to conduct legitimate business and engage in other commercial activities or tourism.[15]

Money cases are also often complex and difficult to prove. In some cases, drug traffickers team up with tax professionals and hide laundered money in legitimate businesses that are difficult to unravel. In others, payments back to DTOs are almost always in the form of currency; that is, hard cash. This currency is generally handled and transported covertly, just as the drugs brought into the US are. Thus, from a law enforcement standpoint, investigations of cash drug proceeds are considered a "contraband" investigation, as opposed to an "asset tracing" investigation. But what if more resources were spent in this direction? After all, a single major bust could pay for all the manpower efforts of law enforcement.

The threat of bulk currency smuggling is further compounded by ineffective inbound interdiction and rampant corruption within Mexico, which allow for the relatively free flow of illicit currency into and throughout the country. To date, efforts by the Calderón administration to crack down on the drug trade, bulk currency smuggling, and money laundering have been extraordinary—and the sacrifices equally high as many law enforcement and military personnel have lost their lives fighting the cartels. As long as profits from the drug trade in the United States represent a substantial share of the Mexican economy, it will be seen as a threat to Mexico's economic infrastructure.

An area where US law enforcement has been successful in investigating and arresting DTO members has been trade-based money laundering. Trade-based money laundering is an alternative remittance system that allows illegal organizations the opportunity to earn, move and store proceeds disguised as legitimate trade. This disguise is moved through by false-invoicing, over-invoicing and under-invoicing commodities that are imported or exported around the world.

Another method being used by DTOs under the same disguise is to provide confusing documentation that is frequently associated with legitimate trade transactions. This method, which is commonly referred to as the Black Market Peso Exchange (BMPE), incorporates purchasing commodities in one country and then transferring them to another country where the commodity is sold and the proceeds remitted back to the DTO as a legitimate business transaction.

But with DTOs using disguises to launder illegal proceeds, why are there only two departments that have investigative resources committed to fighting money laundering? Are the two departments sharing information to better serve law enforcement? The two departments that share a similar mission in stopping illegal proceeds are the DEA and ICE. Both agencies have storied successes. ICE evolved from the Department of Treasury and is now solidly under the umbrella of the DHS, while DEA is an agency within the DoJ. To assist in better coordination between all interested agencies with money laundering enforcement capabilities—notably IRS and CBP—the DEA established the Organized Crime Drug Enforcement Task Force (OCDETF) fusion center in 2006. According to the DEA, the OCDETF fusion center gathers, stores and analyzes all-source drug and related financial investigative information and intelligence to support coordinated, multi-jurisdictional investigations focused on the disruption and dismantlement of the most significant drug trafficking and money laundering enterprises.[16]

In theory, this sounds like a logical plan, but unfortunately there is limited participation with regard to sharing financial information by law enforcement agencies. Thus, one has to ask, are we creating fusion centers for the sake of creating the appearance of cooperation? Or are we not participating in a fusion center because of "law enforcement turf wars?" As we try to answer these questions, the bad guys continue to win.

Chapter Seven

Sharing Drug Intelligence after 9/11

Following the extensive federal investigation of the events of September 11, 2001, the *Final Report of the National Commission on Terrorist Attacks Upon the United States*—the "9-11 Report"—contained an important lesson for our handling and mishandling of national intelligence:

> The U.S. government did not find a way of pooling intelligence and using it to guide the planning and assignment of responsibilities for joint operations involving entities as disparate as the CIA, the FBI, the State Department, the military, and the agencies involved in homeland security.[1]

Since the "9-11Commission" released its report in April 2007, skeptics have questioned whether we are now better off, having exposed the gaps in US intelligence that failed to avert the horrific events of 9/11. Yet this process of investigating, recognizing and addressing our failures in working together is basic to our system of government and enables us to strengthen our intelligence functions by making needed improvements. Consequently, sharing counterterrorism intelligence throughout the federal government has never been better.

But what about sharing drug intelligence? Has sharing drug intelligence caught up with our system for sharing counterterrorism information? In the area of drug intelligence, the federal government still has work to do. Yes, the collectors of intelligence are using better equipment and their training has increased. But is the intelligence that is gathered being shared? Is law enforcement keeping information to itself in order to claim success? Or are there stovepipes that are keeping actionable intelligence from being used to apprehend DTOs?

Generally, each major drug control agency has its own intelligence section. Within the DHS, for example, four agencies have intelligence collectors: Customs and Border Protection (CBP); Immigration and Customs Enforcement (ICE); United States Coast Guard (USCG); and the Intelligence and Analysis unit (IA). The DoJ has the Federal Bureau of Investigation (FBI); the Drug Enforcement Administration (DEA); the Marshals Service; and the Bureau of Alcohol, Tobacco, Firearms and Explosives (ATF). Among these, only the FBI and DEA have dedicated analysts for drugs. In addition, the national intelligence agencies, such as the Office of Director of National Intelligence (ODNI), the Central Intelligence Agency (CIA) and the DoD, have units specializing in counterdrug and terrorism.

Given such a heavy federal presence, one must ask whether this system does not result in a "federalization" of information—that is, keeping information federal and not sharing vital information with state and local officials and law enforcement agencies. Is our way of sharing drug information overly bureaucratic?

Another lesson from the 9-11 Report is that over-classification of certain data that do not need to be classified hinders our ability to maximize the use of sharable intelligence:

> When an intelligence report is first created, its data should be separated from the sources and methods by which they are obtained. The intelligence report should begin with the information that is sharable, but still in meaningful form. Therefore, the maximum number of recipients can access some form of that information.[2]

Traditionally, information shared among federal agencies is classified according to different levels: for official use only; law enforcement sensitive; secret; top secret; and top secret with Sensitive Compartmented Information (SCI). Imagine a scenario where a local police officer stops an individual and runs this person's name through one of a handful of intelligence centers only to be told, "You don't have the appropriate clearance." They cannot tell you who you have or what you have potentially have fallen onto. Why not give the police officer enough information for the officer to draw conclusions?

In response to the 9-11 Report, the intelligence community has been conducting a comprehensive review of collection resources and intelligence requirements that the national intelligence community and law enforcement agencies have arrayed against drug threats to the Southwest border, both within Mexico and in the Southwest region of the United States. The "big three" federal agencies—DHS, DoJ, and DoD—have been moving aggressively to remedy some of the shortcomings in intelligence collection, analysis, and sharing. Yet efforts are needed to better coordinate intelligence operations; develop more efficient means—both technical and organizational—for sharing information between the national intelligence community and law enforcement agencies at all levels; and for providing a comprehensive common operating picture of border threats. There is also a need to improve the coordination of intelligence requirements and collection efforts and expand cooperative efforts of departmental operations and law enforcement, where possible.

FUSION CENTERS

Fusion centers seek to enhance federal, state and local coordination and cooperation to prevent and/or mitigate threats to the homeland. But are there too many or too few fusion centers? What if these fusion centers are devoid of fundamental information? If we have too many fusion centers and have devalued the type of information that is housed, how is there to be any real benefit? Is the country any safer or more prepared with just having more fusion centers? Have we merely created a false sense of security?

Fusion centers with limited information flow or fusion centers that do not have personnel with the appropriate skill sets to understand the information may not provide useful or valuable information. Moreover, as is the case with many fusions centers, if the agencies involved don't buy into a common fusion and prevention philosophy that arguably should accompany fusion centers, then the centers may not be effective. Consider the following examples of beneficial and unsatisfactory uses of drug intelligence fusions centers.

The El Paso Intelligence Center

The El Paso Intelligence Center (EPIC) was established in 1974 in response to a DoJ study entitled, *A Secure Border: An Analysis of Issues Affecting the U.S. Department of Justice.*[3] The study detailed drug and border enforcement, strategy and programs. It recommended an improved operational posture, and it proposed legislative changes to support the recommendations. The study proposed the establishment of a Southwest Border Intelligence Service Center under the direction of the newly created DEA, which was to be staffed by representatives from INS, Customs Service, and DEA. As a result, EPIC was created with a representative from DEA as the Director.

The mission of EPIC is straightforward: support US law enforcement and interdiction components through timely analysis and dissemination of intelligence on illicit drug and alien movements and criminal organizations that are responsible for illegal activities. EPIC also supports specific programs of interest to EPIC member agencies that focus on criminal activity within or en route to the United States on both sides of the US-Mexico border, across the Caribbean, and from other points within the Western Hemisphere.[4]

The mission of EPIC is a sound and viable one. However, since the establishment of DHS and the reorganization of agencies within it in March 2003, some inside the beltway believe that EPIC's mission would be better served under the umbrella of the DHS. The mission of DHS is to secure the homeland and protect it against conventional and unconventional attacks in the United States. DHS also leads response efforts to natural disasters, administers our nation's immigration system, ensures the safety of America's waterways, and interdicts illegal drugs coming across our borders. Effectively performing these functions requires coordination and a focused effort across all levels of government and throughout our country.

Given this mission of DHS, why—other than for historical reasons—is DEA still responsible for cross-border drug and alien interdiction efforts? DEA is a single mission agency with limited statutory authority to apprehend smugglers at the border. But let us not take away from DEA's expertise in enforcement of drug trafficking laws by a typical argument made inside the beltway that focuses more on turf than on substance; namely, security.

An alternative, common sense solution would be to share EPIC equally across DHS, DoJ, DoTrs, and the DoD. EPIC has tremendous value regardless of which agency it reports to. As to the core mission of DHS, it is to protect the borders. No other agency has as huge a mandate or the pressures of day-to-day multiple missions to protect American citizens than does the DHS. However, ICE, the leading investigative agency within DHS does not fully participate in EPIC because ICE already has border intelligence capabilities and does not receive any added value. DEA does not have this capability. So why not share intelligence functions? What type of message are we sending with this lack of cooperation?

Suppose DEA has a case originating from Mexico, which they often do, and is investigating a DTO that traffics drugs through Nogales, Arizona—Arizona's Port of Entry—and then on to a major city destination for drop off. Because ICE is the lead investigator at the border, shouldn't DEA and ICE coordinate their cases though a centralized intelligence center, instead of keeping all the intelligence within one organization? It is also likely that both agencies have overlapping intelligence. Wouldn't law enforcement be better served to take down as many bad guys as possible?

A fusion center should work effectively regardless of which agency flag it raises. As former Secretary of DHS Michael Chertoff said, "Fusion centers are not fly-by-night operations and as a result, if we are asking agencies to invest resources, we need to remain committed."[5] Moreover, an evaluation by the Congressional Research Service indicated that the best method of enhanced coordination is through personnel exchanges.[6] While conferences and Memoranda of Understanding (MOUs) and Memoranda of Agreement (MOAs) between agencies are helpful in building relationships, living in your partners' environment and understanding the demands and limitations of that environment is essential to building mutual trust, understanding and teamwork.[7]

EPIC illustrates the need to improve the coordination of intelligence requirements and collection efforts and to expand cooperative efforts of departmental operations and law enforcement, where possible. To work effectively, fusion centers must allow participating agencies and departments to use their databases, tools, techniques, and procedures to support assigned missions within areas of responsibility while facilitating information sharing with other departments and agencies. This will ensure that the information reaches operational personnel, including those at the state and local levels, in a timely manner.[8]

The High Intensity Drug Trafficking Area Program

Despite the agency turf wars that can hinder law enforcement investigation support, some fusion centers are models of excellence. One model of a fusion center that works well is the High Intensity Drug Trafficking Area (HIDTA).

HIDTAs were established under the Anti-Drug Abuse Act of 1988 and the ONDCP Reauthorization Act of 1998. The latter authorized the Director of ONDCP to designate as HIDTAs specific areas within the United States that exhibit serious drug trafficking problems and that harmfully impact other areas of the country.[9] The HIDTA program provides additional federal resources to those areas to help eliminate or reduce drug trafficking and its harmful consequences. Law enforcement organizations within HIDTAs assess drug trafficking problems and design specific initiatives to reduce or eliminate production, manufacture, transportation, distribution and chronic use of illegal drugs and money laundering.[10]

The HIDTA program helps improve the effectiveness and efficiency of drug control efforts by facilitating cooperation between drug control organizations through resource and information sharing and implementing joint initiatives. HIDTA funds help federal, state and local law enforcement organizations invest in infrastructure and joint initiatives to confront drug-trafficking organizations. Funds are also used for demand reduction and drug treatment initiatives.[11]

Each HIDTA is governed by its own executive board comprised of approximately sixteen members—eight federal members and eight state or local members. These boards facilitate interagency drug control efforts to eliminate or reduce drug threats. The executive boards ensure threat specific strategies and initiatives are developed, employed, supported and evaluated. The HIDTA management structure creates a level playing field among federal, state and local partners who understand all aspects of law enforcement and put the interests of the HIDTA above that of their own home agency for purposes of reducing drug traffic. HIDTA Directors act as neutral brokers for participating agencies and are charged with carrying out the collective policy decisions of their executive boards. What makes the HIDTA program so successful is that it is not dominated by either of the two main federal law enforcement agencies: the DEA or ICE. The funds come from the White House ONDCP and are managed by a cooperative effort of state, local and federal officials.

Another reason for their success is that HIDTAs make it possible to link cases originating with state and local agencies to federal prosecution. HIDTAs act as bridge linking federal, state and local agencies. The HIDTA program has continued to grow because it has been highly successful and capable of uniting a region's law enforcement and criminal justice communities around a shared strategy and goals tailored to regional needs. Since its founding, the program has continually tightened its focus and become more effective and data-driven through its emphasis on threat assessment, intelligence collection and sharing, program evaluation, performance measurement and the use of budgetary authority. Consequently, regional efforts are more highly focused. In addition to these law enforcement functions, the HIDTA program has served as a role model in the development of performance measures and data-tracking systems, such as the nationwide DTO database, which provides real-time tracking of all drug trafficking organizations identified and targeted nationwide by HIDTA task forces.[12]

The highly flexible approach to program planning and administration and continuous support of state and local law enforcement agencies make the HIDTA program a unique platform for both identifying emerging drug threats and developing and implementing responses to them. As of 2008, there were twenty-eight HIDTAs coordinating ongoing task forces to identify and actively target specific drug trafficking organizations having the greatest impact on their regional drug market. They have founded innovative programs, devised and maintained a network of fifty-three regional law enforcement intelligence centers, annually provided continuing education to over 20,000 officers, and established a nationwide secure communications network for intelligence sharing. Approximately fourteen percent of US counties are HIDTA-designated counties; they operate in 45 states, Puerto Rico, the US Virgin Islands, and the District of Columbia.[13]

Finally, another cornerstone of the HIDTA program is the promotion of innovative methods and ideas. The evolution of the HIDTA intelligence subsystem exemplifies this approach. The HIDTA requirement of establishing intelligence centers within each HIDTA and mandating federal, state and local participation has resulted in sharing information and development of intelligence on an unprecedented scale. More importantly, it has accomplished this without the hindrances of turf issues.

Part III

FORTIFYING NEAR
AND DISTANT BORDERS

Chapter Eight

Fighting Drugs along Our Northern Border

Compared with the drugs seizures and violence taking place along our southern border, drug trafficking across our northern border with Canada seldom "makes headlines." Yet our "forgotten border" with Canada is just as vulnerable, if not more, to drug trafficking than our southern border. Our boundary with Canada extends 3,987 miles across both land and water and is often described as the largest open border in the world.[1] This vast border separates two friendly nations with a long history of social, cultural, and economic ties that have contributed to a high volume of cross-border trade and travel. Almost all of Canada's major metropolitan areas are located on or near this international boundary. In fact, ninety percent of Canada's population lives within one hundred miles of the international border.

While legal trade is predominant, criminal networks conduct illicit activities, including the smuggling of drugs, currency, people, and weapons between our two countries. The long porous nature of the US-Canada border provides a multitude of opportunities for traffickers to smuggle illicit drugs and bulk cash. Despite the efforts of US government personnel on the northern border, massive amounts of drugs are smuggled each year through the many crossing points.

Today, Canadian DTOs are exploiting vulnerabilities along the northern border to profit from the lucrative illegal drug trade. Canadian-based Asian gangs control the majority of the flow of drugs across the northern border.[2] In recent years, these groups have increased their drug trafficking activities, and increased trafficking by Asian gangs has led to increasing violence.

69

ECSTASY

Canada produces the world's supply of MDMA, popularly known as "ec-stasy." Between late 2005 and 2006, Canada replaced The Netherlands and, to a lesser extent, Belgium, as the primary supplier of ecstasy destined for the United States.[3] According to a Royal Canadian Mounted Police (RCMP) officer, over 1 million tablets of ecstasy are produced daily in Canada. This officer reports that there are more pill presses than pharmacies in all of Canada.[4] The highest concentration of MDMA labs are found in the provinces of British Columbia and Ontario.

Canada's increased production of ecstasy has had a trickle down effect in the United States, as the US Customs and Border Protection has seen a rise in ecstasy seizures. In 2007 DHS officials seized 8.96 million doses of MDMA along the US-Canada border.[5] As the production of ecstasy has reached unparalleled levels of capacity and sophistication, the MDMA produced in Canada continues to include multiple substances. Most analyses suggest that the "new" ecstasy contains methamphetamine, ketamine, caffeine, pseudo-ephedrine and ephedrine. Of the amounts seized by law enforcement, ap-proximately 22 percent contained these debilitating ingredients.

To some, ecstasy has been described as just a "rave" drug—harmless with no side effects. This couldn't be more inaccurate. Ecstasy is known to cause death. Ecstasy can cause the body to overheat, causing skeletal muscles to break down and organs to fail, leading to an agonizing death. Ecstasy can also cause hyponatremia and hyperthermia by overdose.[6]

Also worrisome is the increased risk of psychological problems as a result of ecstasy use. As low serotonin has been linked to depression and anxiety, it has been suggested that heavy users of ecstasy may be at increased risk of developing long-term psychological problems. Ecstasy has been linked di-rectly to impaired judgment causing confusion, disorientation, panic attacks, insomnia, hallucinations, paranoia and psychotic phenomena.[7]

MARIJUANA

Another drug that is heavily trafficked from Canada into the United States is hydroponic marijuana, also known as "BC Bud." Annual marijuana produc-tion in Canada is estimated to range from 1,399 to 3,498 tons.[8] Production continues to be plentiful in Quebec, Ontario, and British Colombia. Canadian marijuana differs from Mexican marijuana, which also differ from US home-grown cannabis. The psychoactive chemical—delta-9-tetrahydrocannabinol

(THC)—found in marijuana seized in the United States from Canada is present at a high level.[9]

US law enforcement classifies seized marijuana samples in three ways: dill weed, which is very low quality marijuana and includes cannabis growing wild and hemp; commercial grade, which includes buds, leaves, stems and seeds from male and female plants; and sinsemilla, which consists of only the unpollinated flowering tips of female plants. Commercial grade marijuana produced in the United States and Mexico is the most prevalent type of marijuana available throughout the United States. Sinsemilla, on the other hand, is higher in TCH content and commands a higher demand and higher price.[10]

In the United States, the average marijuana confiscated and analyzed showed THC levels of around 5.25 percent in 2004 and 5.59 percent in 2007. In contrast, the THC content of marijuana coming from Canada showed TCH levels of 11.87 percent in 2004 and 11.21 percent in 2007. Both the United States and Canada continue to record abnormally high levels of THC in a limited number of samples, demonstrating that growers in both countries have the capability of producing high TCH marijuana. In 2006, the highest percentage of THC yielded by a marijuana plant seized in the United States was 33 percent, and the highest percentage of THC in marijuana seized in Canada in 2007 was 38 percent.[11] As long as the THC content in marijuana continues to rise, so will the risks associated with marijuana.

The cost of trafficking marijuana into the United States has risen with the demand. In 2007, Canadian and US law enforcement officials witnessed an increased use of private planes to smuggle marijuana into the United States. The planes would rendezvous with off-loaders on the US side of the border, usually on public lands.[12]

COORDINATING ENFORCEMENT ACROSS BORDERS

Although the US-Canada border is the least guarded, with limited law enforcement presence on both sides, both countries have a long history of working well together. Both countries also participate in several bi-national law enforcement task forces that allow information to be shared and operations to be coordinated from both sides of the border. Canadian law enforcement has proven to be an excellent partner against transnational crimes, as has the Government of Canada. Canada's government made a commitment to a new National Anti-Drug Strategy (NADS) supported by their budget in 2007. This strategy takes a balanced approach in reducing both the supply of and demand for illicit substances by giving priority to three objectives: curtailing illicit drug production; reducing precursors and use; and treating illicit drug dependency. This new approach is expected to result in a more focused program for dealing with illicit drugs in Canada. Canada's RCMP will receive additional resources to increase their drug investigation teams and, for the first time, a National Coordinator will oversee activities conducted by special investigative teams in the seven most heavily trafficked areas of Canada.[13]

Similarly, in the United States, additional resources have been allocated in the 2007 and 2008 budgets for northern border interdiction efforts. This allows for an increased federal presence by CBP Border Patrol agents, Field Inspectors, and ICE Special Agents, whether deployed on snowmobiles over snow and ice along the rivers and between islands or new aircraft deployed by CBP Air Wings, which will increase coverage along the border.[14]

In February 2011, Canadian Prime Minister Stephen Harper and US President Barack Obama met and agreed to increase border security and intelligence-sharing among respective law enforcement agencies and to improve cooperation on trade and energy issues.[15] Given the magnitude of drug trafficking, law enforcement and the intelligence community on both sides of the border must coordinate their efforts to disrupt criminal organizations responsible for the cross-border movement of illicit drugs and proceeds and bring the traffickers to justice.

Chapter Nine

Fighting Drugs in Indian Country

Drug trafficking in Indian Country points out the unique vulnerabilities of our northern and southern borders. Approximately 55.7 million acres of land within US borders are held in trust by the US Government for American Indians, Indian Tribes, and Alaska Natives.[1] These lands, collectively referred to as "Indian Country," are under the administration, management, and oversight of the Department of Interior's Bureau of Indian Affairs (BIA). Indian Country includes over 300 federally recognized reservations, upon which nearly 945,000 individuals resided in 2008.[2] A majority of these individuals reside on reservations located in Arizona, New Mexico, Washington, Montana, and South Dakota, which are depicted in Figure 9.1. Approximately fifty-five percent of persons living on federally recognized reservations identified themselves as Native American or Alaskan Native during the 2004 census.[3]

Indian Country constitutes less than three percent of the land area of the United States, but it consists of vast tracts of land, most of which are located in geographically remote areas. Because residents of Indian Country, who make up a relatively small segment of the overall population of the United States, are often geographically isolated from other populations, the societal problems that confront them—including drug abuse—are not as visible as those faced by residents of urban, suburban, or rural areas of the country. Moreover, the isolated nature of Indian Country poses challenges for the efficient provision of public services, such as employment counseling, behavioral and health services, drug dependency treatment, and public safety programs.

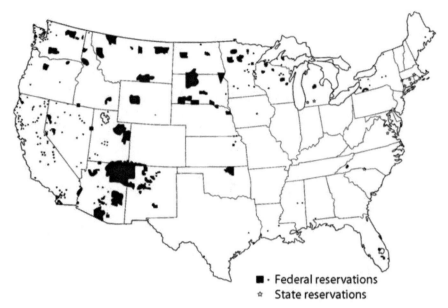

■ · Federal reservations
☆ State reservations

Figure 9.1.   Location of American Indian Reservations in United States, 2006. *Source:* US Department of Interior, Bureau of Indian Affairs.

CHALLENGES FOR LAW ENFORCEMENT

The sizeable area of Indian Country also creates considerable challenges for law enforcement officials in Native American communities. Law enforcement agencies may have jurisdiction over thousands of square miles on reservations, but often have limited personnel and equipment. For example, the BIA had fewer than ten certified drug investigators to cover all of Indian Country in 2007, which means that law enforcement officers must often travel great distances to commit offenders to correctional facilities, sometimes leaving their communities with limited or no police services.[4]

To complicate matters, unemployment on reservations in Indian Country—13.6 percent in 2007 compared to the national rate of 9.8 percent in 2009—is due, in large part, to the limited availability of employment opportunities on reservations.[5] Most Native Americans who are employed work in low-paying jobs with area retailers; social, health, and human service agencies; and tribal offices. Drug trafficking organizations take advantage of the populations living under difficult social and economic conditions, and DTOs are able to infiltrate Native American communities with promises of easy money that is accessible and does not require them to leave the reservation.

In addition to the relative isolation and social and economic conditions on reservations, their location is also a strategic point for DTOs and drug traffickers. DTOs cultivate cannabis on a number of reservations, particularly reservations located in the more isolated Pacific Northwest region, while methamphetamine is reportedly produced on reservations located in the Southwest.

Illicit drugs from Canada are smuggled through reservations adjacent to the US-Canada border, while drugs from Mexico are smuggled through reservations located along the US-Mexico border. Most illicit drugs that are trafficked into and through reservations along our international borders are destined for major drug markets throughout the United States; so reservations that are near large cities may be used as depots for marijuana, cocaine, meth and heroin. Two major reservations highlight these vulnerabilities.

THE ST. REGIS MOHAWK AND AKWESASNE MOHAWK RESERVATIONS

One of the largest reservations along the US-Canada border that has seen an increase in drug trafficking is located along the St. Lawrence River. As depicted in Figure 9.2, the St. Regis Mohawk reservation in the United States and the adjoining Akwesasne Mohawk reservation in Canada straddle the international border between St. Lawrence County and Franklin County in New York and the Canadian provinces of Quebec and Ontario. The geography of the area lends itself to cross-border smuggling, as densely wooded terrain and extensive waterways along the St. Lawrence Seaway shroud the movement of drugs and other contraband. This reservation has become a gateway for trafficking to major cities in the United States, namely New York, Buffalo and Cleveland.

According to law enforcement officials, multi-kilogram quantities of Canadian-produced hydroponic marijuana are trafficked through the reservation unchallenged by tribal law enforcement and then distributed to US cities.[6] Bulk cash then flows back through the reservation and into Canada. Between 2004 and 2006, the DEA seized over 7.5 million in cash and cars from busts on the reservation.[7]

THE TOHONO O'ODHOM NATION

The largest reservation that borders the Republic of Mexico and the United States is the Tohono O'odhom Nation. The Tohono O'odham Nation, with

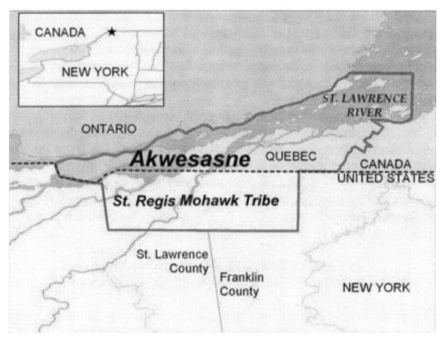

Figure 9.2. Map of the St. Regis Mohawk and Akwesasne Mohawk Reservations.
Source: Akwesasne Housing Authority.

a population of 25,000 in 2006, lies within the Sonoran desert in south central Arizona and extends into Mexico. Sells is the largest city of the Nation
and is its capital. In area, the Tohono O'odhom Nation is the second largest
reservation in the United States. It is made up of four non-contiguous seg-
ments—Tohono O'odham; Gila Bend; San Xavier; and Florence Village—
encompassing an area of 2.8 million acres, roughly the size of Connecticut.

Its size and location along both sides of the international border render it
a wide crossing point where most of the cocaine, marijuana, methamphetamine, and Mexican black tar heroin (MBT) smuggled from Mexico enters
Arizona. Some tribal members live on the Mexican side, and those on the
American side have long freely crossed the border through a few informal
entry points. Seizing upon these informal entry points, drug traffickers try to
enlist tribal members or force them into "cooperation," sometimes stashing
their loads in ramshackle houses dotting the landscape or paying the young to
act as guides. In addition, the vast dessert terrain, along this border adds to the
challenges that law enforcement officers face in safeguarding the US-Mexico
border and stopping illegal drug trafficking across the border.

According to Sheriff Clarence W. Dupnik of Pima County, Arizona, "The hard and real effect for Pima County is that the Mexican border is being strategically increased. Our 132-mile international border is thus augmented by an additional 120 miles of border with Indian Country. While Pima County is home to two International Ports of Entry and hundreds of smuggling routes, the Tohono O'odham Nation increases potential entry points and expands the scope of border enforcement."[8]

THE SHADOW WOLVES

To combat drug trafficking along the Southwest border, and across the Tohono O'odhom Nation, ICE has been using a specialized unit within their patrol division known as the "Shadow Wolves." Since the inception of the Shadow Wolves in 1972 as part of the US Customs patrol unit and the Border Patrol, this unit routinely seizes some 100,000 pounds of illegal drugs per year.[9] What makes the Shadow Wolves an example of how the federal government has stepped up to their part of the bargain of securing America's first families is that the officers must have Native American ancestry, a requirement which is still in place. Members are at least one-quarter Native American, and the current group represents seven tribes, including the Tohono O'odhom.

Using a combination of modern technology and traditional tracking techniques, the Shadow Wolves patrol the 2.8 million acres of the Tohono O'odhom Nation and hone in on drug smugglers who use less-traveled cattle tracks, old wagon-wheel trails and barely formed footpaths to ferry their loads to roads and highways about forty miles from the US-Mexico border. While other law enforcement agencies, including the Border Patrol, use tracking, the Shadow Wolves believe that their experience and native ancestry give them an edge, particularly in Indian Country, where they speak the language of the community, which allows for better communication within the community. According to one Shadow Wolf officer, "Elders of the Tribe are willing to tell us things they know or see that they may not tell another federal agent or officer."[10]

Based on the successes of the Shadow Wolves, they have garnered international attention and have been sent to Kazakhstan, Uzbekistan, Latvia, Lithuania and Estonia to teach ancient tracking skills to customs officials, border guards, and national police in those countries who are training to detect and follow the tracks of people who may be transporting components of weapons of mass destruction. As a result of their contributions to the apprehension and prosecution of drug traffickers here at home, the Shadow Wolves have received death threats over the years. Nonetheless, this unit is a type of deployment that should be used across all Indian tribes infected by drug trafficking as a way to empower honest tribal members to work on the side of law enforcement to stop the addiction of fellow tribal members.

Chapter Ten

The Drug-Terror Nexus

For decades, certain links have existed between drug trafficking and terrorism. Until recently, law enforcement organizations and government officials defined these relationships fairly narrowly, citing examples such as Colombian drug cartels that used terrorist tactics to protect drug routes to further their agendas. Although the United States was a main buyer of illegal narcotics from Colombia, we were not an intended target of Columbian drug violence during the late 1970s and early 1980s. Consequently, the law enforcement community typically addressed drug trafficking and terrorist activities as separate issues.

In the wake of the 9/11 terrorist attacks in New York City, Washington, DC, and Pennsylvania, these two criminal activities have become more visibly intertwined. Since September 11, 2001, it has been acknowledged that a broader range of relationships can and does exist between drug traffickers and terrorist organizations and that these relationships can be quite different from the example provided by Colombian DTOs of the 1980s. It has even been asserted that international drug trade is the most common criminal activity that terrorist organizations pursue to fund their nefarious activities.

THE SOUTH ATLANTIC CONNECTION

Recently, we have seen terrorist organizations from the Middle East working alongside Mexican drug trafficking organizations, furnishing the cartels with weapons and helping them distribute drugs in Europe and the Middle East. Groups like Hezbollah and Hamas have received huge amounts of money from drugs sold to them mainly by Mexican narcotics dealers.

The tripartite border of Brazil, Argentina and Paraguay has become a central point for trafficking cocaine to Europe and other regions of the world, leading to rapidly growing cooperation between Islamic militants operating in North and West Africa and drug lords in Latin America. Drug lords have shifted their supply route from the Caribbean waters to the South Atlantic towards Africa. The sea lanes of the South Atlantic have become a favored route for drug traffickers carrying narcotics from Latin America to West and North Africa, where al Qaeda-related groups are increasingly involved in transporting drugs from South America to Europe.

In addition to serving as transit points for cocaine from Latin America and heroin from Asia, West African countries are also reported to be growing marijuana. In May 2011, police in Sierra Leone seized 3 tons of marijuana valued at $10 million at a location nearly 50 miles from the capital of Freetown. In countries such as Sierra Leone, local law enforcement authorities cite problems such as unemployment, particularly among youth, as creating havens for infiltration by international drug traffickers, which can weaken the rule of law in already fragile countries.[1]

THE TALIBAN CONNECTION

Afghanistan is the major source country for the cultivation, processing, and trafficking of opiates, producing 59 percent of the world's supply of illicit opium in 2006.[2] Because of the country's decimation by decades of warfare, illicit drugs have become a major source of income. Through the taxation of illicit opium production, the Taliban has been able to fund an infrastructure capable of supporting and protecting the Al-Qaeda organization. Accordingly, drugs and terrorism frequently share a common ground of geography, money, and violence.[3]

By 2000, Afghanistan produced more than 70 percent of the world's supply of illicit opium, producing more than 3,656 metric tons. This equaled a potential heroin production of 365 metric tons. An estimate by INTERPOL suggested that ninety percent of the heroin consumed in Europe originates in Southwest Asia, particularly Afghanistan.[4]

The December 2000 International Crime Threat Assessment, produced by an interagency working group chaired by the Central Intelligence Agency (CIA), reported that under predominantly Taliban rule, international terrorists and drug traffickers had been able to operate with impunity in Afghanistan. The Taliban had given sanctuary to renegade Saudi terrorist Osama Bin Laden, allowing him and other terrorist groups to operate training camps in Afghanistan. Bin Laden, in return, had used his extensive wealth and business network to financially support the Taliban. Despite the Taliban's public condemnation of the illicit narcotics industry, virtually all of Afghanistan's opium poppy cultivation and morphine base and heroin processing laboratories are located in Taliban-controlled territory. The Taliban profits from the Afghan drug trade by taxing opium production and drug movements. Reports also linked Osama bin Laden and Al-Qaeda directly to the illicit opium trade. To the extent that income from the trade sustains the Taliban, bin Laden may have benefited at least indirectly as the Taliban was bin Laden's protector.

In 2007, Afghan farmers grew more poppies for opium than ever before, the second year in a row of record production since the United States invaded Afghanistan after the September 11, 2001 attacks. This record illegal drug production in Afghanistan supplies the Taliban insurgency with money and arms. In response, the US-backed government has taken direct action against poppy growers.

One of the biggest problems encountered in the prolonged action against the poppy plant is the Afghan government's prohibition of aerial herbicide spraying by US law enforcement. Instead, opium poppy plants in Afghanistan are destroyed by tractors dragging heavy bars to eradicate the topsoil and pull up the plants, resulting in eradication of only a small proportion of the nearly 430,000 acres under cultivation. It is estimated that for every hectare destroyed, five hectares of poppies are planted; so efforts at eradication lag behind production.

Additionally, the Afghan government believes that thirty percent of families are involved in some form of opium cultivation and production. This production and associated crime and terror undermine security and pose a grave potential threat for massive drug-related corruption at all levels of the government in Kabul.[5] Afghan President Hamid Karzai believes that fighting narcotics is not Afghanistan's business alone, nor can the Afghan government do so by itself unless it receives help from allies and those who join in the belief that narcotics is a common enemy of the whole international community.[6]

The Obama Administration recognizes the need for a comprehensive solution. In President Obama's remarks on the more recent US strategy for Afghanistan, he stressed a need for non-military forms of assistance: "To advance security, opportunity, and justice not just in Kabul, but from the bottom up in the provinces, we need agricultural specialists and educators; engineers and lawyers. That is how we can help the Afghan government serve its people, and develop an economy that isn't dominated by illicit drugs."[7]

The problem in Afghanistan is like the problem in Colombia in terms of resources. However, we have been fighting Colombian drug traffickers for past thirty years and we have only begun fighting the opium trade since 2001.

DRUGS DETER PROGRESS

It is clear that drug trade deters progress toward establishing stable economically independent democracies. In the United States, the following agencies have been tasked to assist in coordinating the federal government's response to the drug-terror nexus (DTX): the DEA International Narco-terrorism Operations Center; the NDIC Drug Terror Unit; the EPIC Crime Terror Nexus Unit; and the CNE DTX Unit. Other agencies with responsibilities include the Defense Intelligence Agency Counter Narcotics Trafficking Office (DIA CNT) and the CIA's Crime and Narcotics Center (CNC). Together, these agencies provide a unified front for stopping Afghan opium from reaching the United States.

As a result, rough estimates show that less than five percent of Afghan heroin or opium reaches the United States.[8] However, this quantity does not deter or detract from the impact of the drug business in Afghanistan, despite a significant US presence in the Middle East. The insurgency is using the drug trade to finance their war on terror against western alliances.[9]

In contrast, terrorist safe-haven countries such as Pakistan and Iran have seen a dramatic shift in narcotics use and chemical dependency in their populations since the US invasion of Afghanistan. As a result, both countries have an epidemic of drug use on their hands but do little to stop the drug trade.[10] It seems inevitable that they will need to do more to support the United Nations' efforts in curbing the illicit trade that goes on daily. As Afghan President Hamid Karzai has repeatedly stated, "If we do not eliminate drugs, drugs will eliminate us."[11]

Epilogue: The Border Challenge

Since the rise of the "drug culture" and the "war on drugs" nearly fifty years ago, the federal mission to stop illegal drugs at America's borders as well as the flow of drug money has been transformed into an increasingly complex border challenge. In the decade since 9/11, this border challenge has called for different strategies along our northern and southern borders and our ports of entry—strategies that are based on our longstanding ties with our neighbors both near and far; their levels of economic development; our respective laws and sanctions for drug trafficking and drug use; the types of illegal drugs being trafficked and the markets for them; and the need for enforcement of collateral threats to security.

Since the terrorist attacks of September 11, 2001, the goals of reducing the types and amounts of illegal drugs entering the United States and stopping the flow of drug money leaving the United States have become increasingly elusive based on our earlier strategies and resources available to achieve them. The flow of drugs and drug money has become so pervasive—and the cost of enforcement and treatment so expensive to governments and taxpayers—that some enforcement officials are now calling for an "end" to the "war on drugs." Why—and just how—these goals have become so elusive, particularly in the decade following 9/11 is, in part, a reflection of the conditions that give rise to terrorism.

According to a commentary on how much the campaign against terrorism has cost the United States, which appeared immediately following the death of Osama bin Laden on May 2, 2011, the authors argue that "the fight against bin Laden has not produced the benefits that accompanied previous conflicts. . . . Meanwhile, our national-security spending no longer drives innovation."[1]

In attempting to assess the economic consequences of this campaign against terrorism, the authors particularly note that:

> Another reason that so little economic benefit has come from this war is that it has produced less—not more—stability around the world. Stable countries, with functioning markets governed by the rule of law, make better trading partners; it's easier to start a business, or tap national resources, or develop new products in times of tranquility than in times of strife.[2]

A lack of stability furthers drug trade. Drug trafficking has increasingly become a lucrative international "business"—one that is economically attractive to people of weaker and poorer nations and one that thrives on drug abuse and addictions to drugs. Unlike legitimate forms of business, drug traffickers pay no business or income taxes on drugs trade, while their illegitimate businesses escalate the costs to legitimate governments and to taxpayers who pay for treating drug addition, fighting crime, and protecting our borders. Drug trafficking organizations also threaten the legal and judicial systems that are established to protect innocent people from harm. A lack of stability in countries beyond our borders directly thwarts the goals of reducing the production and trafficking of illegal drugs and halting the flow of drug money leaving the United States. More indirectly, it also undermines our efforts to reduce the demand for illegal drugs within our borders.

Since 9/11, a paradigm shift has been underway in federal drug enforcement policies in response to both the evolving threats of drug cartels and the ties between drug trade and terrorism. Rethinking the drug war entails an international dialogue that moves beyond the oversimplified debate over treatment versus enforcement—a debate that has viewed the drug war as a domestic issue—to a critique of the demand for illegal drugs by developed countries and the social, political, economic, and environmental conditions that give rise to drug trade and drug markets.

The conditions of instability that give rise to this border challenge call for integrated strategies that address regulatory approaches, the rule of law, and economic development and conflict resolution, which operate in conjunction with law enforcement measures. To further our discussion of this border challenge, we will consider the contributions of policy strategists who are shaping emerging perspectives of drug policy, scholars who offer critiques of legal and regulatory strategies, and proposals of elected officials and interest groups reported in the press.

THE RULE OF LAW

Should Mexico tackle DTOs as the United States confronted organized crime? Under Prohibition, gangs that had limited their activities to gambling and thievery during the early twentieth century were transformed in the 1920s into organized groups of "bootleggers," individuals who illegally brought liquor into the country and sold it to thirsty Americans. Black market bootlegging gangsters, like drug cartels in Mexico, soon became millionaires. Prominent among them was Alphonse "Al" Capone, whose brief career as a Chicago mob boss earned him a reputation as a legendary figure and an income estimated at over $100 million per year.

When the highly profitable bootlegging era officially ended in December 1933 with the ratification of the Twenty-first Amendment, organized crime syndicates focused on other forms of criminal activity, including gambling, loan sharking, prostitution, and drug distribution, as a natural extension of black market bootlegging. Labor racketeering became another lucrative criminal activity. Gangsters worked their way into positions of power in a labor union and then stole from the union's retirement and health funds.

As a result of the rise and proliferation of organized crime in the United States, the US Congress passed the Racketeer Influenced and Corrupt Organization Act of 1970 (RICO) to deem these activities unlawful. Section 1962 of RICO defines the prohibited activities:

> It shall be unlawful for any person who has received any income derived, directly or indirectly, from a pattern of racketeering activity or through collection of an unlawful debt in which such person has participated as a principal . . . to use or invest, directly or indirectly, any part of such income, or the proceeds of such income, in acquisition of any interest in, or the establishment or operation of, any enterprise which is engaged in, or the activity of which affect, interstate or foreign commerce.[3]

RICO has proven to be an extremely powerful tool for convicting organized crime members and has resulted in long prison sentences for convicted criminals. The first RICO convictions of mob bosses or heads of mafia families came in 1980. Numerous other gangsters were convicted under RICO for crimes ranging from operating illegal garbage collection associations to loan sharking and murder. In 1985, the bosses of all five Cosa Nostra crime families in New York City received prison terms of at least one hundred years, dealing a major blow to organized crime.

As a result of three decades of arrests and convictions of Cosa Nostra family members, the American mob's power decreased. Their code of silence—to never testify against another crime member—had been broken by those who testified and received much shorter prison sentences than if they had not cooperated. Thus, a life of organized crime was no longer attractive, and the influence that mobs once held no longer prevails in the United States. Consequently, a considerable number of young people from Cosa Nostra families chose to attend universities and pursue lawful careers.

Currently, Mexico does not have an anti-racketeering statute to go after drug cartels as American law enforcement had against the mob. Should Mexico adopt similar legal tools to use against cartels as the United States did against the mob? Should Mexico also consider reinstituting the death penalty for homicide convictions for crimes committed against elected officials, police, and military forces defending the freedom of the people of Mexico?

In a September 2006 poll that reflects deeply divided but changing views on the death penalty among Mexicans, 55 percent of Mexican adults agreed that allowing the death penalty would help to reduce the level of insecurity in Mexico.[4] However, Mexico has a long history of anti-death penalty views and has not executed anyone for over fifty years. Thus, the prospects of capitol punishment or life in prison are not likely to be seen as a strong deterrent to crime by the present generation of criminals in Mexico.

Capitol punishment and anti-racketeering laws are two examples of US laws that reflect American social and cultural norms with respect to the rule of law. Our differences with Mexico in this regard illustrate an important aspect of the rule of law. In discussing the rule of law, Francis Fukuyama writes:

> The normative dimension of law—that is, people's belief that the law is fundamentally just and their subsequent willingness to abide by its rules—is key to the rule of law. . . . One of the great problems with trying to import modern Western legal systems into societies where they did not exist previously, in fact, is the lack of correspondence between the imported law and the society's existing social norms. Sometimes the importation of legal rules can speed up a process of social change. . . . But if the gap between law and lived values is too large, the rule of law itself will not take hold.[5]

A possible, yet controversial, alternative to "exporting" our capitol punishment laws or "imposing" a RICO statute on our international neighbors is to designate DTOs as FTOs—foreign terrorist organizations—under US law. According to US Representative Michael McCaul (R-Austin) of Texas, "Federal law defines terrorism as an activity that is intended to intimidate a civilian population or to influence the policy of a government by intimidation or to affect the conduct of a government by assassination or kidnapping. . . . In my judgment, the drug cartels fall squarely within this definition." In April 2011, McCaul, who chairs the House Homeland Security Oversight, Investigations, and Management Subcommittee, proposed a bill to the US Congress to expand the definition of terrorism to include DTOs because they present a security threat to both the US and Mexico and because, as McCaul states, it "would give cartels reason to be afraid."[6] Broadening the definition of terrorist organizations to include DTOs is a controversial issue that needs to be deliberated more fully by the US Congress. Only future developments can determine whether it would deter "spillover violence" in the United States.

A REGULATORY PERSPECTIVE

Given recent trends in public opinion regarding medicinal uses of marijuana and drug-related violence in Mexico, a number of past political leaders—including the former President Ernesto Zedillo of Mexico, former US Secretary of State George Shultz, and former UN Secretary General Kofi Annan—have endorsed a June 2011 report by the Global Commission on Drug Policy in what has been described as "a watershed moment." The report emphasizes public health over criminalization in an effort redirect what is increasingly viewed as a failed drug policy. It essentially calls for "decriminalization and experiments with legal regulation."[7] Proponents of decriminalization anticipate the report will garner additional bipartisan political support for decriminalizing marijuana in the United States.

A similar declaration was issued by a group of organizations in June 2010, in advance of an international conference on HIV (Human Immunodeficiency Virus) in Austria in July 2010. This declaration by organizations working on HIV and drug policies called for a "science-based public health approach" to illegal drug use. The declaration claims that "criminalization of illicit drug users is fueling the HIV epidemic and has resulted in overwhelmingly negative health and social consequences." The organizations claim that enforcement has been "expensive and futile." Alternatively, they support drug policies based on "proven and evidence-based interventions . . . not ideology."[8]

Whether the United States should relinquish its drug laws and enforcement mechanisms in the way it repealed the prohibition of alcohol in earlier era is a question for policy analysts. Paul Stares notes that "the legalization alternative typically surfaces when the public's anxiety about drugs and despair over existing policies are at their highest." He cautions that "drug legalization is not a public policy option that lends itself to simplistic or superficial debate." While calling for "a fundamental assessment of whether our existing responses to this problem are sufficient to meet the likely challenges ahead," Stares cautions that

> jettisoning nearly a century of prohibition when the putative benefits remain so uncertain and the potential costs are so high would require a herculean leap of faith. Only an extremely severe and widespread deterioration of the current drug situation, nationally and internationally is likely to produce the consensus—again, nationally and internationally—that could impel such a leap. Even then the legislative challenge would be stupendous. The debate over how to set the

conditions for controlling access to each of a dozen popular drugs could consume the legislatures of the major industrial countries for years.[9]

Mexico's 2008 decision to decriminalize hard drugs, including methamphetamines, cocaine, LSD and heroin, is likely to be a test. Will it prove both naïve and impractical to assume this policy approach will somehow ease drug violence in Mexico and across our southern border? Are new drug users likely to generate more money for already powerful cartels, which will enable the cartels to buy more guns and ammunition, to bribe Mexican officials, and to undermine efforts to maintain stability? Once again, many innocent citizens of Mexico and US border towns risk paying the heaviest price.

Will it also send the wrong message to Mexico's citizens? Mexico's drug laws allow addicts to be treated free of cost. Yet in a country of 109 million people with a drug addiction rate of over 30 percent during 2004–2009, Mexico has only 100 clinics to treat a reported 4.5 million addicts. This policy option presents a tremendous challenge: Will treatment outpace drug use and thereby reduce demand for drugs? If not, is the Mexican government prepared to allocate additional funds to pay for additional drug treatment clinics?[10]

Unwittingly, Mexico's policy has sent a distorted message to the United States and the international community about its commitment to stop drugs from imploding in their country, despite the US pledge of $150 million dollars in 2009 to fight Mexican DTOs. Although the Mexican government finds that drug trafficking is a shared problem with United States, owing to the US appetite for drugs, Mexico may now become the destination vacation for drug users. Gen. Barry McCaffrey, drug czar under the Clinton Administration, warned in February 2009 that President Calderón's government was in danger of losing control of some areas of the country; that millions of Mexicans could seek refuge from violence in the USA; that Mexico ranked alongside Iran as a top security risk to the United States; but that our southern neighbor had now made drug use legal.[11]

Expressing astonishment at the idea of decriminalizing hard drugs such as cocaine, heroin and methamphetamines, Dr. James Califano, Jr., former Secretary of Health, Welfare and Education under the Carter Administration, contends, "Drugs are not dangerous because they are illegal; they are illegal because they are dangerous."[12] Decriminalizing a drug changes the legal borders we have placed around a certain drug to prevent access to it and to keep it "off-limits."

In the case of marijuana, the dangers of marijuana were called into question by the Shafer Commission in March 1972, long before states began decriminalizing the use of marijuana for medicinal purposes. After nearly forty years, federal regulation of marijuana may be changing. Governor Christine "Chris" Gregoire of Washington, one of the first states to decriminalize the use of marijuana for medicinal purposes, is proposing to work with governors from other states to seek reclassification of marijuana under the federal Controlled Substances Act. According to this proposal, marijuana would be declassified as a Schedule 1 drug (having no medical utility) and reclassified as a Schedule 2 drug (having lower potential for abuse and some medical utility). This regulatory approach to reclassifying marijuana at the federal level has been prompted by the risk and continuing uncertainty of federal prosecution in states dispensing marijuana for medical purposes and the possibility of jeopardizing the state laws that currently permit its medicinal use—not because of new evidence of marijuana's dangers to health or rejection of the state laws.[13]

If such a proposal succeeds, the reclassification of marijuana under federal law would present an object lesson in how drug policies are enacted and amended: The borders around illegal drugs are defined at the interface of science, law, politics, economics and culture.

A POST-CONFLICT MODEL

Our attempts to eradicate illegal drugs such as opium or marijuana have taught us that a direct approach to interdiction may undermine the security of our homeland, disrupt the natural environment, and have destabilizing effects on other societies. Since 9/11, our attempts to curb the opium supply from Afghanistan by eradicating poppy fields at a critical time in that country's transition to a rule of law have empowered insurgents or terrorists and turned farmers and poppy growers against the newly formed Afghan government and the fragile stabilizing forces within their country. As Vanda Felbab-Brown, a Fellow in the Foreign Policy Program at The Brookings Institution, notes, "Policies toward suppressing labor-intensive illegal economics in poor countries are deeply counterproductive from the perspective of the counter-insurgency" because they "increase the political capital, the legitimacy and popular support that accrues to belligerent groups that sponsor the illicit economy."[14]

Similarly, attempts to eradicate marijuana crops in the United States have pushed growers not only to find more remote or inaccessible locations to grow marijuana but also to challenge our values and priorities for protecting the environment and preserving national parkland. By growing marijuana in remote areas of national parks, growers have usurped national parkland for illegal profit without regard for the environmental consequences. Others have moved cultivation indoors not only to avoid scrutiny by drug enforcement agents but also to produce a steadier supply and to increase the potency of the product to command a higher price.

In Afghanistan and other parts of Asia and the Middle East as well as Mexico and even the United States, drug interdiction efforts must be integrated with economic and political aims to support stability. Interdiction may be more effective if it aims at minimizing the economic and political harm to local populations through legitimate economic alternatives to cultivation of illicit opium poppies or marijuana. According to Felbab-Brown:

> Governments can prevail against militants despite the nexus of illegal economies and the immense . . . multifaceted power that belligerents derive from them. . . . if they adopt a proper policy toward the illicit economy, if they abstain from hurting large amounts of the population, if they adopt policies that enable the population to transition via security and development of a legal economy . . . from marginalization into being a legal and respected citizen of the state. And ultimately, the best way to make sure that the nexus does not threaten states is to make sure that illegal economies and conflict never meet.[15]

An example of this approach to supporting economic and political stability is a public and private investment program for the US-Mexico border. In June 2001, the US Chamber of Commerce proposed a plan for investing in "combined improvements in infrastructure, security, immigration policies and trade" to establish a secure border and a prosperous economic relationship with Mexico. In presenting the plan, Tom Ridge, former Secretary of DHS and Chairman of the US Chamber's National Security Task Force, observed, "Our security and our prosperity intersect at the border."[16]

Since 9/11, a paradigm shift has been underway in federal drug enforcement policies in response to the evolving threats of drug cartels and the ties between drug trade and terrorism. Rethinking the drug war entails an international dialogue that moves beyond the debate over treatment versus enforcement—a debate that has oversimplified the drug war as a domestic issue—to a critique of the demand for illegal drugs by developed countries and the social, political, economic, and environmental conditions that give rise to illegal drug trade and drug markets. Strategies that address regulatory approaches, the rule of law, economic development and conflict resolution are needed to address the conditions of instability that give rise to illegal drug trade and to the demand for drugs. Working in conjunction with law enforcement efforts, long-term integrated strategies are needed to meet the common challenges of controlling drug trade and securing our borders. Borders will continue to play a strategic role in controlling illegal drugs, and the legal and regulatory borders we establish around drugs will continue to be enacted and amended at the interface of science, law, politics, economics and culture.

Acronyms and Abbreviations

9/11	September 11, 2001
AFI	Agencia Federal de Investigación of Mexico
AMO	Air and Marine Operations
AMOC	Air and Marine Operations Center
ATF	Bureau of Alcohol, Tobacco, Firearms and Explosives
ATVs	All Terrain Vehicles
BADC	Bureau of Drug Abuse Control, Food and Drug Administration
BCI	Border Coordination Initiative
BIA	Bureau of Indian Affairs, US Department of Interior
BIC	Border Interdiction Committee
BIWG	Bilateral Interdiction Working Group
BMPE	Black Market Peso Exchange
BNDD	Bureau of Narcotics and Dangerous Drugs, US Department of Justice (founded 1968; replaced by DEA)
BSA	Bank Secrecy Act
C3I	Control and Communication and Intelligence
CBP	Customs and Border Protection, US Department of Homeland Security
CDICG	National Counterdrug Intelligence Coordination
CDX	Counterdrug Intelligence Executive Secretariat
CIA	Central Intelligence Agency
CMIR	Currency and Monetary Instrument Report
CNC	Crime and Narcotics Center, Central Intelligence Agency
CNE	Office of Counternarcotics Enforcement, US Department of Homeland Security
CNT	Counter Narcotics Trafficking Office, Defense Intelligence Agency

CPB	Customs and Border Protection, US Department of Homeland Security
CTAC	Counter Drug Technology Assessment Center
DEA	Drug Enforcement Administration, US Department of Justice (founded 1973)
DHS	US Department of Homeland Security
DIA	Defense Intelligence Agency
DoD	US Department of Defense
DoJ	US Department of Justice
DoS	US Department of State
DoT	US Department of Transportation
DoTrs	US Department of Treasury
DTO	Drug Trafficking Organizations
DTX	Drug Terror Nexus
EPIC	El Paso Intelligence Center
FDA	Food and Drug Administration
FBI	Federal Bureau of Investigation
FinCEN	Financial Crimes Enforcement Network
FTOs	Foreign Terrorist Organizations
GCIP	General Counterdrug Intelligence Plan
GPRA	Government Performance and Results Act of 1993
HALCON	Operation Falcon (joint border air patrol between the US and Mexico)
HIDTA	High Intensity Drug Trafficking Area
HIV	Human Immunodeficiency Virus
IA	Intelligence and Analysis unit, DHS
ICDE	Interagency Crime and Drug Enforcement
ICE	Immigration and Customs Enforcement, DHS
IG	Inspector General
INCSR	International Narcotics Control Strategy Report (of US Department of State)
INS	Immigration and Naturalization Service
IRS	Internal Revenue Service
IWG	Interagency Working Group
JIATF	Joint Interagency Task Forces
JTF-N	Joint Task Force-North
JTF-S	Joint Task Force-South
K-9 Units	Canine Units
LACDD	Latin American Commission on Drugs and Democracy
MBT	Mexican Black Tar Heroin
MDMA	3,4-Methylenedioxymethamphetamine (commonly known as "Ecstasy")
Meth	methamphetamine
MOAs	Memoranda of Agreement
MOUs	Memoranda of Understanding
MPA	Maritime Patrol Aircraft

NAFTA	North American Free Trade Agreement (enacted 1993)
NADS	National Anti-Drug Strategy (of Canada)
NCDPP	National Counter Drug Planning Process
NDIC	National Drug Intelligence Center
NDCS	National Drug Control Strategy (an annual report by the ONDCP)
NICCP	National Interdiction Command and Control Plan
NIDA	National Institute on Drug Abuse
NMLS	National Money Laundering Strategy
NORML	National Organization for the Reform of Marijuana Laws (founded 1970)
NSA	National Security Agency
NSC	National Security Counsel
OCDETF	Organized Crime Drug Enforcement Task Force, US Department of Justice
ODALE	Office of Drug Abuse Law Enforcement (founded 1972; replaced by DEA)
ODNI	Office of Director of National Intelligence
OFAC	Office of Foreign Assets Control
OFC	OCDETF Fusion Center
ONDCP	Office of National Drug Control Policy, The White House (founded 1988)
OPBAT	Operation Bahamas, Turks & Caicos
PDD	Presidential Decision Directive
POE	Port of Entry
PLDCC	Public Land Drug Control Committee
RCMP	Royal Canadian Mounted Police (of Canada)
RICO	Racketeer Influenced and Corrupt Organizations Act (enacted 1970)
SAODAP	Special Action Office for Drug Abuse Prevention
SCI	Sensitive Compartmented Information
SOD	Special Operations Division, Drug Enforcement Administration
State INL	US Department of State, Bureau of International Narcotics and Law Enforcement Affairs
SWB	Southwest Border Area of the United States
TECS	Treasury Enforcement Communications System
THC	delta-9-tetrahydrocannabinol (the psychoactive substance in the cannabis plant or marijuana)
UAV	Unmanned Aerial Vehicle
UNODC	United Nations Office on Drugs and Crime
US	United States of America
USCG	United States Coast Guard, US Department of Homeland Security
USIC	United States Interdiction Coordinator

Chronology: Legislative Milestones and Popular Events in Controlling Illegal Drugs, 1911–2011

This chronology highlights legislative milestones in controlling illegal drugs as well as popular events that have influenced public awareness of drug use and drug policy issues in our society. It focuses on developments in federal drug control strategies and agencies during the past one hundred years. It includes policies and events that reflect the shifting emphases on enforcement versus treatment as strategies for controlling illegal drugs, specifically opiates, cocaine, marijuana, and methamphetamine. With respect to enforcement, it includes landmarks in the development and modification of mandatory federal sentencing guidelines for possession and distribution of illegal drugs, which serve as an underpinning for enforcement. It also includes domestic and international events that reflect the broader context of the federal government's ongoing mission to control illegal drugs.[1]

1911 March 12   *The New York Times* publishes an article entitled, "Uncle Sam is the Worst Drug Fiend in the World," quoting "Opium Doctor" Hamilton Wright—the United States Opium Commissioner; American delegate to the International Opium Commission meeting in Shanghai, China, in February 1909; and Chief of the American delegation to the Opium Conference in The Hague, in May 1911—who describes American medical practices of prescribing opium as "deplorable;" notes that the "awakening of interest in our own great [opium] problem" is a result of international attention to opium trade; characterizes drug habits of Americans as a "National curse;" and opines that abuse of cocaine is a "direct incentive to crime" and "pre-eminent" in America, compared with other countries[2]

1914	Harrison Narcotics Tax Act restricts the sale of morphine and later cocaine
1919 October 28	US Congress overrides a veto of the National Prohibition Act ("Volstead Act") by President Woodrow Wilson, establishing the enabling legislation for the 18th Amendment and prohibiting the sale, manufacture and transport of alcohol
1920s	Prohibition creates a black market for beverage alcohol; mafia organize bootlegging; crime rates increase; respect for law is undermined; marijuana use is popular and legal
1930 June 14	Federal Bureau of Narcotics established within the Department of Treasury, the only law enforcement agency that could regulate commerce and goods
1933 February 20	US Congress proposes the 21st Amendment (repealing Prohibition under the 18th Amendment) by a two-thirds majority of both houses and chooses ratification by state conventions under Article V of the Constitution
1933 December 5	21st Amendment is ratified, officially ending Prohibition effective December 15, 1933
1936	International Narcotic Education Association issues a pamphlet entitled, "Marihuana or Indian Hemp and Its Preparations," in which it reports that marijuana is known as the "killer drug" because it can lead to crimes of assault and murder and is called "loco weed" because it can produce insanity[3]
1937 August 2	Marijuana Transfer Tax Act attempts to destroy the hemp industry, a competitor to the paper and synthetic fiber industries, by taxing the sale of marijuana and imposing strict sentences for breaking the law
1939–1944	In view of widespread use of marijuana and conflicting opinions of the effects of smoking marijuana, the Committee on Public Health Relations of the New York Academy of Sciences convenes a subcommittee to study its effects at the request of Mayor Fiorello La Guardia; the Mayor's Committee on Marihuana—the "La Guardia Committee"—conducts both a clinical study of the effects of smoking marijuana and a sociological study of marijuana use in New York City; in its report, the Committee concludes that "smoking marihuana does not lead to addiction in the medical sense of the word" and that "publicity concerning the catastrophic effects of marihuana smoking in New York City is unfounded"[4]

1951	Boggs Act establishes mandatory minimum sentences for possession of marijuana, cocaine and opiates
1954 November 27	President Dwight D. Eisenhower establishes the Interdepartmental Committee on Narcotics to coordinate anti-drug efforts among federal agencies
1956 July 18	Narcotic Control Act stiffens penalties for possession of illegal drugs
1960s	Recreational drug use increases in the United States; the marijuana leaf becomes a symbol of the counterculture
1968	Bureau of Narcotics and Dangerous Drugs (BNDD) consolidates the Bureau of Narcotics from the DoT and the Bureau of Drug Abuse Control from the Food and Drug Administration within the DoJ to allay turf wars
1969 August	Dr. Robert DuPont finds a high rate of heroin use among persons entering jail in the District of Columbia, leading to an association between crime and heroin use; initiates methadone treatment for heroin addicts
1969 August 16–18	Woodstock Music Festival, Bethel, New York
1969 September 21	Operation Intercept, designed to reduce marijuana smuggling from Mexico to the United States, disrupts travel across the Southwest border without seriously curtailing the flow of marijuana
1970	National Organization for the Reform of Marijuana Laws (NORML) is founded to advocate for decriminalization of marijuana
1970	US Congress enacts the Racketeer Influenced and Corrupt Organization Act (RICO) as a tool for prosecuting and convicting organized criminals
1970 March 11	President Richard M. Nixon announces an expanded federal program to treat drug abuse
1970 September 18	Jimi Hendrix, considered the greatest electric guitarist, dies of an overdose of sleeping pills and alcohol in London at age 27
1970 October 4	Janis Joplin, a pioneer blues musician, dies in Hollywood, California, of an overdose of heroin at age 27
1970 October 27	Comprehensive Drug Abuse Prevention and Control Act consolidates previous federal drug laws; the Controlled Substances Act establishes five "schedules" for regulating drugs based on their medicinal value and potential for addiction

1970 December 21	Elvis Presley, "the king of rock and roll," visits The White House to help convey the president's message against drug abuse
1971 May	US Congressmen Robert Steele and Morgan Murphy issue a bipartisan report on the "heroin epidemic" among US military personnel in Vietnam
1971 June 17	President Richard M. Nixon declares "war on drugs," identifying drug abuse as "public enemy number one in the United States;" creates the Special Action Office for Drug Abuse Prevention (SAODAP) headed by Dr. Jerome Jaffe, a methadone treatment specialist
1971 July 3	Jim Morrison, a rock musician, dies in Paris, France, at age 27 of unspecified cause
1971 September	Operation Golden Flow: US military forces initiate testing for heroin use among servicemen; 4.5 percent of servicemen test positive
1972 January	By Executive Order, President Richard M. Nixon establishes the Office of Drug Abuse Law Enforcement (ODALE) within the DoJ to provide federal assistance to state and local law enforcement agencies to detect, arrest and prosecute street-level heroin traffickers "who profit from the misery of others"[5]
1972	United States and France break-up heroin smuggling by the "French Connection" in southern France
1972	Shadow Wolves become a unit of the US Customs Service; by agreement with the Tohono O'odham Nation, federal law enforcement agents who are of at least one-fourth Native American ancestry are allowed on the Native American lands adjacent to the 76-mile border the Tohono O'odham Nation shares with Mexico; using traditional Native American tracking skills and modern technology, the Shadow Wolves patrol this remote desert area, which is one of the most dangerous drug trafficking and illegal immigration routes from Mexico to the United States[6]
1972 March 22	National Commission on Marihuana and Drug Abuse (the "Shafer Commission") recommends decriminalizing marijuana and focusing efforts on preventing and treating use of "hard" drugs

1973 July 1	Drug Enforcement Administration (DEA) is founded as a "super agency" within the DoJ; consolidates agents from BNDD, Customs, CIA and ODALE; consolidation of these enforcement agencies supports an emphasis on enforcement of drug laws by the criminal justice system
1974	National Institute on Drug Abuse (NIDA) is established to advance efforts to treat and prevent drug abuse through a scientific understanding of addiction
1975	Miami, Florida becomes known as the "drug capital of the Western Hemisphere" as US Customs seizes increasing quantities of cocaine; illegal drug trafficking becomes a $10 billion wholesale industry, the largest in the state; and competition between Cuban and Columbian drug traffickers for control of the market escalates into "cocaine wars"[7]
1975 September	President Gerald Ford issues a White Paper on Drug Abuse that recommends reducing the supply and demand for those drugs that are more dangerous to individuals and society; marijuana is of lower priority than heroin, amphetamines, and barbiturates
1975 November 22	Medellin Massacre: after Columbian police seize 600 kilos of cocaine at the Cali Airport, a vendetta by Columbian drug traffickers leaves 40 people dead in one weekend
1976	As a presidential candidate, Jimmy Carter campaigns in favor of decriminalizing marijuana
1977 August 16	Elvis Presley dies of a heart attack at age 42 in Memphis, Tennessee, after a history of prescription drug abuse
1979	Following his release from federal prison, Carlos Enrique Lehder-Rivas purchases property on Norman Cay, a Bahaman island about 210 miles from the coast of Florida, for use as a hub for transporting cocaine between Columbia and the United States, as part of a plan to transform cocaine trafficking by transporting mega quantities in small private planes and by forming an alliance among manufacturers and distributors of cocaine, known as the Medellin Cartel[8]
1979 July 11	Drug violence in South Florida—marked by a shooting at the Dadeland Mall, the largest shopping center in Florida—is linked to Colombian drug traffickers operating in the United States[9]

1981–1982	Pablo Escobar, one of the richest and most violent members of the Medellin Cartel, gains notice by his tactics of corrupting or intimidating Columbian law enforcement and government officials
1981	Ratification of a bilateral agreement between the United States and Columbia to extradite suspected Columbian drug traffickers for prosecution in the United States becomes a turning point for Columbian cartels by making it harder to escape prosecution
1982	Lucrative deal between Pablo Escobar and Panamanian Gen. Manuel Noriega allows Columbian cocaine traffickers to ship cocaine through Panama
1982 January 28	South Florida Drug Task Force formed in response to increased drug-related violence in Miami; other regional task forces follow
1982 March 9	Seizure of a single shipment of 3,906 pounds of cocaine, valued at over $100 million wholesale, at the Miami airport, demonstrates the scope and order of magnitude of the Medellin Cartel's operations compared with small-scale traffickers; reaction prompts increased emphasis on law enforcement and support for stiffer penalties for drug dealers and users
1984	First Lady Nancy Reagan visits Longfellow Elementary School in Oakland, California, to warn students of the dangers of drug abuse; in response to a student's question, she advises students to "Just say, 'No'" when they are offered drugs; "Just Say No" becomes the slogan of the Reagan administration's anti-drug campaign
1984 November 6	A large marijuana smuggling operation is discovered in a joint DEA-Mexican raid on a complex in the Chihuahua dessert in Mexico
1985 January 5	Columbia extradites four drug traffickers to Miami
1985–1986	Highly addictive crack cocaine becomes available in the United States and at lower cost than powder cocaine
1986 June 19	Len Bias, a promising basketball star, dies from an overdose of cocaine at age 22 in Riverdale, Maryland
1986 October 27	Anti-Drug Abuse Act increases enforcement, education and treatment; imposes mandatory minimum penalties for drug offenses, which lead to racial disparities between convicted offenders
1986 November 18	Federal grand jury in Miami indicts three members of the Medellin Cartel—Pablo Escobar, Carlos Lehder and Jose Gonzalo Rodriguez Gacha—under the RICO statute

1987 May 28	Columbian Supreme Court annuls the extradition treaty with the United States after threats by drug traffickers
1988 February 5	Federal grand jury in Miami indicts Panamanian Gen. Manuel Noriega for drug trafficking by allowing the Medellin Cartel to launder money and manufacture cocaine in Panama
1988	US Senate Subcommittee on Narcotics, Law Enforcement and Foreign Policy reports that DoS funds and personnel supported drug trafficking by Contras in Nicaragua
1989	Office of National Drug Control Policy (ONDCP) is established to centralize the coordination of drug policy; President George H. W. Bush appoints William Bennett as Director
1989 Dec 20	Operation Just Cause: United States invades Panama to capture and arrest Gen. Manual Noriega for drug trafficking
1990 January 25	President George H. W. Bush proposes a $1.2 billion increase in the drug control budget; increases DoD spending for drug control by 50 percent
1992	NIDA becomes part of the National Institutes of Health
1993 July–2009	Under the "Bill" Clinton Administration, the position of Director of ONDCP—"Drug Czar"—is elevated to cabinet-level status
1993 November 17	North American Free Trade Agreement (NAFTA) is enacted to increase trade between the United States and Mexico; increased trade makes it harder for US Customs to control illegal drug traffic at the United States-Mexican border
1994	Senator Joseph Biden's Omnibus Crime Bill includes a provision to impose the death penalty for drug kingpins, making federal drug offenses the legal equivalent of murder and treason
1995	After the US Sentencing Commission reports on racial disparities in the sentencing of crack versus powder cocaine offenders, the US Congress overrides recommendations to amend federal sentencing guidelines to reduce racial disparities
1996	By means of a ballot initiative, California becomes the first state to decriminalize the use of marijuana when it is medically prescribed; marijuana remains an illegal drug under federal policy

1998 May	Operation Casablanca: the largest money-laundering probe in US history leads to indictments against Mexican and Venezuelan banks and to arrests; Mexican and Venezuelan governments view the undercover operation as a threat to their national sovereignty
1998 July	United States and Mexico sign the Brownsville Agreement, agreeing to inform each other about cross-border law enforcement operations
2000 August	Plan Columbia: United States provides $1.3 billion in aid to equip and train Columbian military forces in counternarcotics activities, making Columbia one of the largest recipients of US foreign aid at the time; as an extension of the "war on drugs," its law enforcement approach is controversial because it gives anti-narcotics aid to the Columbian military and uses aerial fumigation to eradicate coca crops
2001 September 11	Terrorist attacks on the World Trade Center in New York City and the Pentagon in Arlington, Virginia, and an averted attack on Washington, DC, prompt the "war on terror"
2002 November 25	Homeland Security Act establishes the Department of Homeland Security (DHS) to protect the United States against terrorism or domestic emergencies
2003 March 1	In the largest US government reorganization since the establishment of the DoD in 1947, 22 federal agencies with air, land or sea border control or law enforcement functions are transferred to and reorganized within the DHS, including the US Customs Service (from DoTrs), which includes the Shadow Wolves unit; Immigration and Naturalization Services (from DoJ); and the US Coast Guard (from DoT)
2005	DEA begins operations in Afghanistan to disrupt production and distribution of opium in what is described as "a not-so-noticed war within a war" in which drugs and terrorism are linked[10]
2007 March 15	In the largest drug cash seizure in history, DEA in cooperation with Mexican officials seizes $207 million from brokers who provided Mexican cartels with chemical supplies to make methamphetamine; the seizure reflects both the global market for "meth" and the ability of cartels to shift production outside the United States in response to attempts to curtail production within the United States[11]

2007 March 18   Operation Panama Express: With Panamanian, DEA
                     and interagency cooperation, US Coast Guard seizes
                     over 40,000 pounds of cocaine worth over $500 million
                     from the Gatun, a Panamanian ship, off the southwest
                     coast of Panama; as the largest maritime drug seizure
                     in US history, it illustrates both the "mentality of impu-
                     nity" among drug traffickers and the lucrative nature of
                     drug trafficking[12]

2007 December 10   In deciding *Kimbraugh v. United States,* the Supreme
                     Court of the United States strikes down mandatory fed-
                     eral sentencing guidelines for crack cocaine[13]

2008 March–June   References to "Mexico's Drug War" appear in head-
                     lines of major US newspapers and online wire service
                     reports[14]

2008 June 30   DoS launches the Merida Initiative to combat drug traf-
                     ficking and crime with a three-year commitment of aid
                     for law enforcement and judicial reforms in Mexico and
                     Central America

2008   As a presidential candidate, Barack Obama campaigns
                     in favor of eliminating the disparity in mandatory sen-
                     tencing for crack and powder cocaine offenses

2008 December   Economist Jeffrey A. Miron estimates that decriminal-
                     izing illegal drugs in the United States would save $44
                     billion in enforcement costs and increase tax revenues
                     by $32 billion annually; such estimates have particular
                     sway with segments of the public at a time of financial
                     stress and rising federal debt

2009 May 13   Under the Barack H. Obama administration, Drug Czar
                     Gil Kerlikowske aims to remove barriers to treatment
                     within the criminal justice system in order to break
                     the cycle of illegal drug use, crime and incarceration,
                     signaling a shift in policies in favor of treatment and
                     enforcement that targets high priority offenders; the
                     Director of ONDCP no longer has cabinet-level status[15]

2009 June 25   Michael Jackson, "the king of pop," dies in Los Ange-
                     les, California, at age 50 of an overdose of prescription
                     drugs

2009 October 26   Three DEA agents are killed in a helicopter crash in
                     Afghanistan following a firefight with suspected Tali-
                     ban drug traffickers, becoming the first DEA casual-
                     ties since the DEA began operations in Afghanistan in
                     2005[16]

2010 March 17	US Senate unanimously passes a bill to reduce the sentencing ratios (established in 1986) for crack cocaine versus powder cocaine; reducing the sentencing ratios is expected to reduce racial disparities in sentences for cocaine offenses, refocus law enforcement resources on high-level traffickers, and restore a measure of confidence in the criminal justice system[17]
2010 May 10	FY 2010 National Drug Control Budget increases funds for prevention and treatment of drug abuse; drug control strategy also emphasizes enforcement along the Southwest border and on Native American lands
2010 July 28	Fair Sentencing Act amends the 1986 Anti-Drug Abuse Act to reduce disparities in mandatory sentences for crack versus power cocaine offenses by reducing the ratio from 100 to 1 to about 18 to 1 and by eliminating the five-year mandatory minimum sentence for first-time offenders convicted of possession of crack[18]
2011 February 4	Canadian Prime Minister Stephen Harper and US President Barack Obama agree to increase border security and intelligence sharing among respective law enforcement agencies and to improve cooperation on trade and energy issues[19]
2011 February 15	While on assignment to the ICE Attaché at the US embassy in Mexico City, Special Agent Jaime Jorge Zapata is killed, and Agent Victor Avila is injured, in an attack by suspected members of a Mexican drug cartel; the loss of a fellow law enforcement officer in the line of duty resonates among US law enforcement personnel as a brazen affront to US immigration and drug enforcements efforts[20]
2011 February	United States escalates intelligence-gathering in cooperation with the Mexican government and law enforcement agencies by using unarmed aerial surveillance over Mexican territory to locate and track drug traffickers[21]
2011 March 3	Mexican President Felipe Calderón and US President Barack Obama meet and agree to continue aerial surveillance over Mexican territory; this step is viewed as an effort on the part the US president to bridge a standoff with Mexico by responding to the "common threat" of transnational criminal activities aggravated by illegal weapons and US demand for illegal drugs, and as a sign of pragmatism on the part of Mexico's president

in balancing nationalistic sentiments, legal authority, social discontent, and threats of instability in agreeing to greater intervention by the United States[22]

2011 March 9   Eric Clapton, one of the greatest guitarists in rock history, auctions his collection of guitars to raise funds for a drug and alcohol treatment center he founded in Antigua, West Indies, drawing popular attention to fighting drug addictions through medically supervised treatment[23]

Notes

PREFACE

1. Reflecting the tangled history of tribal sovereignty, the prosecution of certain felonies committed by Native Americans on tribal lands falls under federal, rather than tribal, jurisdiction under the Major Crimes Act of 1885, and its amendments, 18 U.S.C. §1153. Based on the territorial location of tribal lands, these cases now constitute "a major part of the practice of federal criminal law in several very large federal districts, such as Arizona, New Mexico, South Dakota and Montana, and a significant part in others, such as Minnesota, Nevada and Washington." Native American Advisory Group. *Report of the Native American Advisory Group*, November 4, 2003, 2, http://www.ussc.gov/NAAG/ NativeAmer.pdf (accessed March 11, 2010).

2. The term *Indian Country* is used throughout this book in its legal sense, defined under 18 U.S.C. § 1151 to include:

a) all land within the limits of any Indian reservation under the jurisdiction of the United States Government, notwithstanding the issuance of any patent, and, including rights-of-way running through the reservation, (b) all dependent Indian communities within the borders of the United States whether within the original or subsequently acquired territory thereof, and whether within or without the limits of a state, and (c) all Indian allotments, the Indian titles to which have not been extinguished, including rights-of-way running through the same.

http://frwebgate.access.gpo.gov/cgi-bin/getdoc.cgi?dbname=2006_uscode &docid=18USC1151 (accessed March 11, 2010).

3. *See*: James Pinkerton and Susan Carroll, "As Border Emphasis Changes, Drug Cases Show Drop," April 14, 2007, http://www.chron.com/disp/story.mpl/ front/4714304.html (accessed March 13, 2010).

INTRODUCTION

1. This account of early federal drug laws is based on the following sources: Lana D. Harrison, Michael Backenheimer and James A. Inciardi, "Cannabis Use in the United States: Implications for Policy," in Peter Cohen and Arjan Sas (eds.) *Cannabisbeleid in Duitsland, Frankrijk en de Verenigde Staten*. Amsterdam: Centrum voor Drugsonderzoek, Universiteit van Amsterdam, 237-47, http://www.cedro-uva. org/lib/harrison.cannabis.05.html (accessed May 12, 2010); "United States 14 Jul 2009 Nixon war on drugs 40 years ago," July 14, 2009, http://www. newsahead.com/ preview/2009/07/14/united-states-14-jul-2009-nixon-war-on-drugs-40-years-ago/index.php (accessed May 10, 2010); Tom Head, "History of the War on Drugs," http:// civilliberty. about.com/od/drugpolicy/tp/War-on-Drugs-History-Timeline.htm (accessed May 10, 2010).

2. Lana D. Harrison, Michael Backenheimer and James A. Inciardi, "Cannabis Use in the United States: Implications for Policy," 237-47.

3. According to one source, monopolistic interests aimed at preventing industrial uses of hemp, the fibrous part of the cannabis plant, also played a role. Hemp was a less expensive substitute for paper pulp, used to produce newspaper, and also competed with nylon, a new synthetic fiber. *See* "War on Drugs," http://en.wikipedia.org/ wiki/War_on _Drugs (accessed May 10, 2010).

4. Lana D. Harrison, Michael Backenheimer and James A. Inciardi, "Cannabis Use in the United States: Implications for Policy," 237-47.

5. An example of trafficking narcotics to finance political opposition parties resisting "noble cause" military operations is found in a brief account of narcotics smuggling by the Communist Party in Japan during the Occupation. *See* Crawford F. Sams, *Medic: The Mission of an American Military Doctor in Occupied Japan and Wartorn Korea*. New York: M.E. Sharpe, 1998, chapter 17 on Narcotics Control, 153-56, 288n4.

6. "Woodstock 1969-08/15/1969-08/28/1969," http://www.woodstock.com/1969-festival/ (accessed May 17, 2010).

7. The author of this memorandum is unidentified, but related White House documents indicate Dwight L. Chapin and H. R. Halderman arranged the meeting and Egil "Bud" Krogh attended the meeting and wrote a summary of the meeting for the President's file. Memorandum for the President, Subject: Meeting with Elvis Presley, December 21, 1970, The White House, Washington, DC, 2, http://www.gwu.edu/~ nsarchiv/nsa/ elvis/docs/doc04.pdf (accessed May 12, 2010).

8. The rates reported here are based on Bureau of the Census population data and Federal Bureau of Investigation, *Uniform Crime Reports for the United States*, annual, and are published in the following sources: US Bureau of the Census, *Statistical Abstract of the United States, 1976*, 97th ed. Washington, DC: Government Printing Office, 153, http://www2.census.gov/prod2/statcomp/documents/1976-03.pdf (accessed May 10, 2010); The Disaster Center, "United States Crime Index Rates Per 100,000 Inhabitants" (under "United States Crime Rates 1960–2008,") http://www. disastercenter. com/crime/ uscrime.htm (accessed May 10, 2010).

9. "Thirty Years of America's Drug War: A Chronology," http://www.pbs.org/wgbh/pages/ frontline/shows/drugs.cron (accessed May 10, 2010).

10. "Thirty Years of America's Drug War: A Chronology," http://www.pbs.org/wgbh/pages/ frontline/shows/drugs.cron (accessed May 10, 2010).

11. National Commission on Marihuana and Drug Abuse, "Marihuana: A Signal of Misunderstanding," March 22, 1972, Chapter V: Marijuana and Social Policy, http://www.druglibrary.org/schaffer/library/studies/nc/ncrec1_17.htm (accessed March 27, 2010).

12. The personal prejudices and ideological views that underlay this decision by President Nixon have been made public through the release of the presidential tapes. For a critique of Nixon's response to the Shafer Commission report, *see*: Kevin Zeese, "Once-Secret "Nixon Tapes" Show Why the U.S. Outlawed Pot," March 21, 2002, http://www.alternet. org/story/12666/?page=entire (accessed May 15, 2010); "Nixon Tapes Reveal Twisted Roots of Marijuana Prohibition," http://www.csdp.org/news/news/nixon.htm (accessed May 15, 2010).

13. Lana D. Harrison, Michael Backenheimer and James A. Inciardi, "Cannabis Use in the United States: Implications for Policy," 237-47.

14. National Commission on Marihuana and Drug Abuse, "Marihuana: A Signal of Misunderstanding," March 22, 1972, Chapter V: Marijuana and Social Policy, http://www.druglibrary.org/schaffer/library/studies/nc/ncrec1_17.htm (accessed March 27, 2010).

15. United Nations Office on Drugs and Crime, *World Drug Report 2005*, Vol. 1, Vienna, Austria: United Nations ODC, 2005, Figure 1, 127, 129-30, http://www.unodc.org/pdf/ WDR_2005/volume_1_web.pdf (accessed May 20, 2010); Paul B. Stares, *Global Habit: The Drug Problem in a Borderless World*, Washington, DC: Brookings Institution Press, 1996, 2.

16. MDMA (3,4-Methylenedioxymethamphetamine, commonly known as "ecstasy"), crack cocaine, methamphetamine ("meth"), LSD, heroin and PCP (phencyclidine) are also prevalent but at lower rates of use than marijuana, prescription narcotics and cocaine. National Drug Intelligence Center, *National Drug Threat Assessment 2009*, 2008-Q0317-005, Washington, DC: US Department of Justice, December 2008, 17, 33, 70-71.

17. National Drug Intelligence Center, *National Drug Threat Assessment 2009*, December 2008, 1-2, 65, 74.

CHAPTER 1: THRESHOLDS OF CONCERN

1. *See:* The Brookings Institution Latin American Initiative, "Drugs and Democracy: Toward a Paradigm Shift," Washington, DC, April 6, 2009, 6, 8, 25, 42, http://www. brookings.edu/~/media/Files/events/2009/0406_drugs_democracy/20090406_ drugs_democracy.pdf (accessed March 21, 2010).

2. For example, the National Organization for the Reform of Marijuana Laws (NORML) carefully avoids using the term *legalize*. Instead, the expression "removal

of state-level criminal penalties" is used to refer to the changes in state laws that decriminalize the use, possession or cultivation of marijuana for medical purposes. *See*: National Organization for the Reform of Marijuana Laws, "Active State Medical Marijuana Programs," http://norml.org/index.cfm?Group_ID=8088 (accessed March 21, 2010).

3. Paul Stares, "Drug Legalization?: Time for a Real Debate," The Brookings Institution, Spring 1996, http://www.brookings.edu/articles/1996/spring_crime_stares. aspx?p=1 (accessed March 23, 2010); Jeffrey A. Miron, "The Budgetary Implications of Drug Prohibition," December 2008, 2, http://proxychi.baremetal.com/leap.cc/dia/ miron-economic-report.pdf (accessed March 27, 2010); The Brookings Institution Latin American Initiative, "Drugs and Democracy: Toward a Paradigm Shift," April 6, 2009, 12, 25, http://www.brookings.edu/~/media/Files/events/2009/0406_drugs_ democracy/ 20090406_drugs_democracy.pdf (accessed March 21, 2010).

4. Jean Kalata, *Medical Uses of Marijuana: Opinions of U.S. Residents 45+*, Washington, DC: American Association of Retired Persons, December 2004, http:// assets.aarp.org/ rgcenter/post-import/medical_marijuana.pdf (accessed March 23, 2010).

5. In this poll, the term *legalizing* appears to be used interchangeably in the sense of *decriminalizing*. ABC News/Washington Post Poll: Medical Marijuana, "High Support for Medical Marijuana," January 18, 2010, http://abcnews.go.com/images/ PollingUnit/ 1100a3 MedicalMarijuana.pdf (accessed March 21, 2010).

6. In addition to the 14 states that have passed laws removing state-level criminal penalties for the use, possession or cultivation of marijuana for medical purposes as of January 21, 2010, the State of Maryland and the District of Columbia have also passed reforms in this direction. The Maryland state legislature passed a law in 2003 that allows an affirmative defense of medical necessity for marijuana use, which would mitigate the penalties under state law. In such cases, the maximum penalty would be a $100 fine.

In 1998, voters in the District of Columbia passed a ballot measure to decriminalize the use of marijuana for medical purposes. The ballot measure was approved by 69 percent of voters, which is the largest margin of approval in any jurisdiction to date. Approval of the measure by the US Congress was required because the District of Columbia is a federal district and not a state. Barriers to the implementation of this initiative were not approved by Congress until December 8, 2009, when the DC City Council was finally given the authority to promulgate rules regulating the dispensing of marijuana for medical purposes in the District of Columbia. The rules are expected to be issued by the end of 2010. National Organization for the Reform of Marijuana Laws, "Active State Medical Marijuana Programs," http://norml.org/index.cfm?Group_ID=8088 (accessed March 21, 2010). *See also*: Drug Policy Alliance Network, "Reform in Washington, DC," http://www.drug policy.org/statebystate/ washingtondc/ (accessed March 23, 2010); Committee on Appropriations. Summary: FY2010 Financial Services and General Government Appropriations Consolidated Appropriations Bill, December 8, 2009, 4, http://www. appropriations.senate.gov/ news.cfm?method=news.view&id=6281cfe0-2f15-4fdd-b048-a8f092f4c9f4 (accessed March 27, 2010).

7. Researchers found similar increases in the use of the prescription narcotics Vicodin and OxyContin by adolescents since 2008. According to Nora Volkow, Director of the NIDA, the perception of risk in the case of prescription drugs involves falsely reasoning that it is less dangerous to get high on prescription drugs "because they are endorsed by the medical community."

The reported use of methamphetamine ("meth") by adolescents has continued to decline since 1999. This trend in meth use by adolescents is consistent with the increased awareness of the risks associated with meth, which were graphically communicated in a media campaign aimed at preventing its use and by the controls placed upon the over-the-counter medication pseudoephedrine, the main ingredient in methamphetamine, in 2005. David N. Goodman, "Study Shows Pot More Popular Among Teenagers," December 14, 2009, http://abcnews.go.com/IS/wireStory?id=9330773 (accessed March 18, 2010); Centers for Disease Control and Prevention, Trends in the Prevalence of Marijuana, Cocaine, and Other Illegal Drug Use: National Youth Risk Behavior Survey (YRBS), 1991-2007, http://www.cdc.gov/HealthyYouth/yrbs/pdf/yrbs07_us_drug_use_trend.pdf (accessed March 27, 2010).

8. National Drug Intelligence Center, *National Drug Threat Assessment 2009*, December 2008, figure 12, 18-19. *See also:* "Report: Marijuana Potency Rises," June 12, 2008, http://www. usatoday.com/news/health/2008-06-12-marijuana_N. htm?csp=34 (accessed March 21, 2010).

9. National Drug Intelligence Center, *National Drug Threat Assessment 2009*, December 2008, 18-19.

10. *See*: National Institute on Drug Abuse. *Marijuana: Facts for Teens*. NIH Pub. 08-4037 Bethesda, MD, Revised March 2008, http://www.drugabuse.gov/Marij-Broch/Marij intro.html (accessed March 21, 2010).

11. Carrie Johnson, "U.S. Eases Stance on Medical Marijuana," October 20, 2009, http://www.washingtonpost.com/wp-dyn/content/article/2009/10/19/AR2009101903638.html (accessed March 21, 2010); David Stout and Solomon Moore, "U.S. Won't Prosecute in States That Allow Medical Marijuana," October 20, 2009, http://www.nytimes.com/2009/10/20/us/20cannabis.html?_r=1&pagewanted=print (accessed March 21, 2010); Office of National Drug Control Policy, Comments on DOJ Guidelines, October 20, 2009, http://www.whitehousedrugpolicy.gov/news/press09/dk_medmj _comments.html (accessed March 2, 2010).

12. Interview with Gil Kerlikowske, "Q&A With the New Drug Czar," *The Wall Street Journal*, May 14, 2009, http://online.wsj.com/article/SB124233331735120871. html (accessed May 18, 2010).

13. Office of National Drug Control Policy. *National Drug Control Strategy FY 2011 Budget Summary*. Washington, DC, 2010, 1, http://www.ondcp.gov/publications/policy/11budget /fy11budget.pdf (accessed May 17, 2010).

14. Gary Fields, "White House Czar Calls for End to 'War on Drugs,'" *The Wall Street Journal*, May 14, 2009, http://online.wsj.com/article/SB124225891527617397. html (accessed May 18, 2010).

15. Andrew Selee, David Shirk and Eric Olson, "Five Myths About Mexico's Drug War," *The Washington Post*, March 28, 2010, http://www.washingtonpost.com/wp-dyn/ content/article/2010/03/26/AR2010032602226_pf.html (accessed March 29,

2010); Keven Casas-Zamora, "Drugs and Democracy: Toward a Paradigm Shift," April 22, 2009, Washington, DC: The Brookings Institution, http//www.brookings. edu/opinions/2009/0422_drugs_and_democracy_casaszamora.aspx?p=1 (accessed March 23, 2010).

16. Mark Potter, "Border Officials Fear Growing Mexican Drug War," May 23, 2008, http://fieldnotes.msnbc.msn.com/archive/2008/05/23/1053308.aspx (accessed March 21, 2010); William Booth, "Mayhem Crosses the Border with Informers," August 27, 2009, http://www.washingtonpost.com/wp-dyn/content/article/2009/08/26/ AR2009082603768. html?sid=ST2009082603806 (accessed March 16, 2010); Ioan Grillo and Tim Padgett, "A Major Blow to Mexico's Masters of Meth," October 23, 2009, http://www.time.com/ time/nation/article/0,8599,1932030,00.html (accessed March 16, 2010); E. Eduardo Castillo, "Slaying of Drug War Hero's Family Shocks Mexico," December 22, 2009, http://abcnews.go.com/International/ wireStory?id=9400795 (accessed March 16, 2010).

17. Mark Potter, "Mexican Drug War 'Alarming' U.S. Officials" June 25, 2008, http://worldblog.msnbc.msn.com/archive/2008/06/25/1166487.aspx (accessed March 21, 2010).

18. Ioan Grillo and Tim Padgett, "A Major Blow to Mexico's Masters of Meth," October 23, 2009, http://www.time.com/time/nation/article/0,8599,1932030,00.html (accessed March 16, 2010).

19. The Brookings Institution Latin American Initiative, "Drugs and Democracy: Toward a Paradigm Shift," Washington, DC, April 6, 2009, 6, http://www.brookings. edu/~/media/Files/events/2009/0406_drugs_democracy/20090406_drugs_democracy.pdf (accessed March 21, 2010).

20. The Brookings Institution Latin American Initiative, "Drugs and Democracy: Toward a Paradigm Shift," Washington, DC, April 6, 2009, 7-8, 11, http://www. brookings.edu/~/media/Files/events/2009/0406_drugs_democracy/20090406_drugs_ democracy.pdf (accessed March 21, 2010).

21. Carlotta Gall, "Opium Harvest at Record Level in Afghanistan," September 3, 2006, http://www.infowars.com/articles/ww3/afghanistan_opium_harvest_soars_record_levels.htm (accessed March 17, 2010).

22. Robert H. Reid and Heidi Vogt, "DEA Agents Among 14 Americans Dead in Afghanistan," October 26, 2009, http://abcnews.go.com/International/ wireStory?id=8914054 (accessed March 16, 2010).

23. Keven Casas-Zamora, "Drugs and Democracy: Toward a Paradigm Shift," April 22, 2009, Washington, DC: The Brookings Institution, http//www.brookings. edu/opinions/2009/0422_drugs_and_democracy_casaszamora.aspx?p=1 (accessed March 23, 2010).

CHAPTER 2: ORGANIZING
AND FINANCING DRUG ENFORCEMENT

1. Matthew B. Robinson and Renee G. Scherlen, *Lies, Damned Lies, and Drug War Statistics: A Critical Analysis of Claims by ONDCP* (Albany, NY: State University Press, 2007), 19-28.

2. Matthew B. Robinson and Renee G. Scherlen, *Lies, Damned Lies, and Drug War Statistics*, 63-71.

3. To provide for consistency in reporting and comparability over time, the amounts reported for FY 2002 and FY 2003 have been adjusted using the methodology introduced in FY 2004. Office of National Drug Control Policy. *National Drug Control Strategy FY 2011 Budget Summary*. Washington, DC, 2010, table 3, 17, http://www.ondcp.gov/ publications/policy /11budget/fy11budget.pdf (accessed May 17, 2010).

4. Office of National Drug Control Policy. *National Drug Control Strategy FY 2011 Budget Summary*, table 2, 16, A1. *See also* Office of National Drug Control Policy, *National Drug Control Strategy: FY 2003 Budget Summary* (Washington, DC: The White House, February 2002); *FY 2005 Budget Summary* (March 2004); *FY 2006 Budget Summary* (February 2005).

5. Bureau of Justice Statistics, *Major City Crime Arrests*. (Washington, DC: US Department of Justice, 2007), 1-3.

6. Office of National Drug Control Policy. ONDCP Mission Statement (Washington, DC: The White House), http://www.ondcp.gov (accessed 2009).

7. Office of National Drug Control Policy. ONDCP Mission Statement.

CHAPTER 3: POLITICAL LEADERSHIP FOR DRUG POLICY

1. Office of National Drug Control Policy. ONDCP Authorizing Language (1988). (Washington, DC: The White House), http://www.ondcp.gov (accessed June 2009).

2. Office of National Drug Control Policy. ONDCP Authorizing Language (1988).

3. Office of National Drug Control Policy. *National Drug Control Strategy FY 1994*. (Washington, DC: The White House, 1993).

4. Office of National Drug Control Policy. *National Drug Control Strategy FY 1997*. (Washington, DC: The White House, 1996).

5. *See* Dallas Courrege, "Goodbye to OPBAT," *Soldiers Magazine,* August 2007, http://findarticles.com/p/articles/mi_m0OXU/is_8_62/ai_n27339248/?tag=mantle_skin;content accessed (June 4, 2011).

6. Theresa Cook, "US Coast Guard Makes Biggest Cocaine Bust in US History," http://abcnews.go.com/US/story?id=2970799 (accessed March 16, 2011).

7. Office of National Drug Control Policy, *National Drug Control Strategy: FY 2004 Budget Summary* (Washington, DC: The White House, 2003).

8. The DoJ's guidelines stop short of advocating decriminalization of marijuana. Nor can ONDCP take positions contrary to laws passed by Congress; therefore, it cannot advocate for decriminalization of marijuana, which is regulated under the Controlled Substances Act. Carrie Johnson, "U.S. Eases Stance on Medical Marijuana," October 20, 2009, http://www.washingtonpost.com/wp-dyn/content/article/2009/10/19/AR2009101903638. html (accessed March 21, 2010); David Stout and Solomon Moore, "U.S. Won't Prosecute in States That Allow Medical Marijuana," October 20, 2009, http://www.nytimes.com/2009/10/20/us/20cannabis. html?_r=1& pagewanted=print (accessed March 21, 2010); Office of National Drug Control Policy, Comments on DOJ Guidelines, October 20, 2009, http://www

.whitehousedrugpolicy.gov/ news/press09/dk_medmj_comments.html (accessed March 2, 2010).

9. Mike Baker, "States reassess marijuana laws after fed warnings, May 3, 2011, http://news.yahoo.com/s/ap/us_medical_marijuana_feds (accessed May 3, 2011).

10. Interview with Gil Kerlikowske, "Q&A With the New Drug Czar," *The Wall Street Journal*, May 14, 2009, http://online.wsj.com/article/SB124233331735120871. html (accessed May 18, 2010); Office of National Drug Control Policy. *National Drug Control Strategy FY 2011 Budget Summary*. Washington, DC, 2010, 1, http://www.ondcp.gov/ publications/policy/11budget /fy11budget.pdf (accessed May 17, 2010).

11. Jim Abrams, "Congress passes bill to reduce disparity in crack, powder cocaine sentencing, http://www.washingtonpost.com/wp-dyn/content/article/2010/07/28/AR2010072802969.html?hpid=topnews (accessed March 16, 2011); National Association of Criminal Defense Lawyers, "Crack Cocaine Sentencing Reform," http://www.nacdl.org/public.nsf/PrinterFriendly/Crack?openDocument (accessed March 16, 2011); Drug Policy Alliance, "US Senate Unanimously Approves Bill to Reduce Crack/Power Cocaine Sentencing Disparity," http://www.drugpolicy.org/news/pressroom /press release/pr031710.cfm (accessed March 16, 2011).

12. Jessica Gresko, "New law on crack cocaine could apply to old cases," May 31, 2011, http://news.yahoo.com/s/ap/20110531/ap_on_re_us/us_crack_hopeful_prisoners (accessed June 1, 2011).

13. Text: Remarks by PM Stephen Harper and US President Barack Obama, February 4, 2011, http://www.canada.com/business/Text+Remarks+Stephen+Harper+President +Barack+Obama/4227060/story.html (accessed March 19, 2011); Chris Hawley, "At northern border, agents fight drug war on ice," http://news.yahoo.com/s/ap/20110214/ ap_on_re_us/us_forgotten_border (accessed February 14, 2011).

14. Ginger Thompson and Mark Mazzetti, http://www.nytimes.com/2011/03/16/world/americas/16drug.html (accessed March 18, 2011); *see also* John M. Ackerman, "Obama's Mexico Standoff," http://www.the dailybeast.com/blogs-and-stories/2011-03-02/obamas -mexico-standoff-calderon-visits-washington-amid-unrest/full/ (accessed March 2, 2011).

15. House Committee on Government Reform, Subcommittee on Criminal Justice, Drug Policy and Human Resources. 2006 Congressional Drug Control Budget and Policy Assessment: A Review of the 2007 National Drug Control Budget and the 2006 National Drug Control Strategy, 109th Cong., 2nd sess., 2006, 1-136.

16. House Committee on Government Reform, Subcommittee on Criminal Justice, Drug Policy and Human Resources. *2006 Congressional Drug Control Budget and Policy Assessment*, 101.

17. House Committee on Government Reform, Subcommittee on Criminal Justice, Drug Policy and Human Resources. *2006 Congressional Drug Control Budget and Policy Assessment*, 12-16.

18. House Committee on Government Reform, Subcommittee on Criminal Justice, Drug Policy and Human Resources. *2006 Congressional Drug Control Budget and Policy Assessment*, 29-32.

CHAPTER 4: TURF WARS EMPOWER DRUG TRAFFICKERS

1. Lou Holtz, *Winning Every Day: The Game Plan for Success* (New York: Harper Collins Publisher, 1999), 168.

2. 31 U.S.C. § 1115. The Government Performance and Results Act of 1993 (GPRA) (P.L. 103-62).

3. Carnevale Associates. A Report: Budget Emphasizes Supply Reduction (Washington, DC, 2009)1-16.

CHAPTER 5: FIGHTING DRUGS AND
VIOLENCE ALONG OUR SOUTHWEST BORDER

1. National Drug Intelligence Center. *Southwest Drug Threat Assessment* (Washington, DC: US Government Printing Office, 2007), 1-59.

2. National Drug Intelligence Center. *Southwest Drug Threat Assessment*, 11-12.

3. Government Accountability Office. "US Assistance Has Helped Mexican Counternarcotics Efforts but Tons of Illicit Drugs Continue to Flow to the US" (Washington, DC: US Government Printing Office, June 2007), 1-81.

4. Government Accountability Office. "US Assistance Has Helped Mexican Counternarcotics Efforts but Tons of Illicit Drugs Continue to Flow to the US," 20-27.

5. Government Accountability Office. "US Assistance Has Helped Mexican Counternarcotics Efforts but Tons of Illicit Drugs Continue to Flow to the US," 26-37.

6. Government Accountability Office. "US Assistance Has Helped Mexican Counternarcotics Efforts but Tons of Illicit Drugs Continue to Flow to the US," 43-61.

7. Government Accountability Office. "US Assistance Has Helped Mexican Counternarcotics Efforts but Tons of Illicit Drugs Continue to Flow to the US," 39-44.

8. William Booth, "Mexico weighs options as lawlessness continues to grip Ciudad Juarez," *The Washington Post*, December 27, 2009, A1-A2.

9. William Booth, "Mexico weighs options as lawlessness continues to grip Ciudad Juarez," A1.

10. Cook, Colleen W. Congressional Research Service Report for Congress: Mexico's Drug Cartels (Washington, DC: US Government Printing Office, October 16, 2007), 1-24.

11. *See, e.g.*, Andrew Selee, David Shirk and Eric Olson, "Five Myths About Mexico's Drug War," *The Washington Post*, March 28, 2010, http://www.washington-post.com/wp-dyn/content/article/2010/03/26/AR2010032602226_pf.html (accessed March 29, 2010); Mark Potter, "Border Officials Fear Growing Mexican Drug War," May 23, 2008, http://fieldnotes.msnbc.msn.com/archive/2008/05/23/1053308.aspx

(accessed March 21, 2010); Mark Potter, "Mexican Drug War 'Alarming' U.S. Officials" June 25, 2008, http://worldblog.msnbc.msn.com/archive/2008/06/25/1166487. aspx (accessed March 21, 2010).

12. Cook, Colleen W. Congressional Research Service Report for Congress: Mexico's Drug Cartels, October 16, 2007), 9-18.

13. Archibald, Randal, "Mexican Drug Cartel Violence Spills Over US," *New York Times*, March 9, 2009, http://www.nytimes.com (accessed April 20, 2011).

14. Killerbrew, Robert and Bernal, Jennifer, "Crime Wars: Gangs, Cartels and US National Security," Center for a New Security, March 2010, p 1-84. http://www. cttso.gov/publications/CNAS_CrimeWars_ KillebrewBernal (accessed April 2011).

15. Simon, D, "Mexican Cartels Running Pot Farms in US National Forest," CNN News, August 8, 2008.

16. Simon, D, "Mexican Cartels Running Pot Farms in US National Forest."

17. Senate Committee on Homeland Security. *Southern Border Violence: Homeland Security Threats, Vulnerabilities, and Responsibilities*, 111th Cong., 1st sess., Washington, DC, March 25, 2009.

18. "Mexico's Drug War: Number of Dead Passes 30,000," *BBC News*, August 17, 2010.

19. Killerbrew and Bernal, "Crime Wars: Gangs, Cartels and US National Security,"

20. Brady McCombs and Tim Stellar, "Border seen as unlikely terrorist crossing point," *Arizona Daily Star*, June 7, 2011, http://azstarnet.com/news/local/border/article_ed932aa2-9d2a-54f1b930-85f5d4ccc9a8.html (accessed June 9, 2011).

21. Government Accountability Office. Report on Drug Control: "US Assistance Has Helped Mexican Counternarcotics Efforts but Tons of Illicit Drugs Continue to Flow to the US," 34-35.

22. "Terror on the Border," *El Paso Times,* August 17, 2008.

23. Ibid.

24. Office of National Drug Control Policy. *US National Southwest Counternarcotics Strategy.* (Washington, DC: US Government Printing Office, 2009), 1-20.

25. Office of National Drug Control Policy. *US National Southwest Counternarcotics Strategy*, 6-7.

26. US Department of Homeland Security. *Office of Counternarcotics Enforcement Annual Report to Congress.* (Washington, DC: US Department of Homeland Security, April 2008), 4-6.

27. House Appropriations Committee Subcommittee on Homeland Security. Statement of Marcy Foreman, Director of Operations, US Immigration and Customs Enforcement. 111th Cong., 1st sess., Washington, DC, March 10, 2009.

28. Office of National Drug Control Policy. *US National Southwest Counternarcotics Strategy*, 5-7.

29. Alexandra Olson, "US Releases $214 Million to Aid Mexico Drug Fight," Associated Press, September 2, 2009.

CHAPTER 6: INTERCEPTING
THE BUSINESS OF ILLEGAL DRUGS

1. Office of National Drug Control Policy. *National Drug Control Strategy FY 2008*, (Washington, DC: The White House, February 2007), 1-56.

2. Naylor, R. T., *Wages of Crime: Black Markets, Illegal Finance, and the Underworld*, (Ithaca, NY: Cornell University Press, 2002), 138.

3. Decker, Scott, and Margaret Townsend Chapman, *Drug Smugglers on Drug Smuggling: Lessons from the Inside*. (Philadelphia, PA: Temple University Press, 2008), 1-154.

4. Naylor, R. T., Wages of Crime: Black Markets, Illegal Finance, and the Underworld, 45-70.

5. "Mexican Drug Cartels: The Evolution of Violence," STRATFOR Global Intelligence, October 15, 2007, 43-45.

6. Decker, Scott, and Margaret Townsend Chapman, *Drug Smugglers on Drug Smuggling: Lessons from the Inside*, 51-53.

7. National Drug Intelligence Center. *Money Laundering Threat Assessment* (Washington, DC: US Government Printing Office, 2006), 1-4.

8. Farah, Douglas, *Money Laundering and Bulk Cash Smuggling: Challenges for the U.S. Mexico Border*, International Assessment and Strategy Center, June 19, 2009, 1-26.

9. Farah, Douglas, *Money Laundering and Bulk Cash Smuggling: Challenges for the U.S. Mexico Border*, International Assessment and Strategy Center, June 19, 2009, 14-16.

10. Farah, Douglas, *Money Laundering and Bulk Cash Smuggling: Challenges for the U.S. Mexico Border*, International Assessment and Strategy Center, June 19, 2009, 12-13.

11. Statement by Administrator Karen P. Tandy on Two Hundred and Seven Million in Drug Money Seized in Mexico City, http://www.justice.gov/dea/pubs/pressrel/pr032007.html (accessed March 19, 2011).

12. US Department of State. *2007 International Narcotics Control Strategy Report.* (Washington, DC: US Government Printing Office, 2007), 63-70.

13. The Merida Initiative. http://www.state/meridainitiative.gov (accessed 2008).

14. Farah, Douglas, *Money Laundering and Bulk Cash Smuggling: Challenges for the U.S. Mexico Border*, International Assessment and Strategy Center, June 19, 2009, 24.

15. Farah, Douglas, *Money Laundering and Bulk Cash Smuggling: Challenges for the U.S. Mexico Border*, International Assessment and Strategy Center, June 19, 2009, 24.

16. US Department of Justice, Organized Crime Drug Enforcement Task Force. Drug Fusion Center Mission Statement. http://www.dea.gov (accessed 2006).

CHAPTER 7: SHARING DRUG INTELLIGENCE AFTER 9/11

1. National Commission on Terrorist Attacks Upon the United States. *The 9-11 Commission Report: Final Report of the National Commission on Terrorist Attacks Upon the United States*, Official Government Edition. (Washington, DC: US Government Printing Office, April 2007, 19-21.

2. National Commission on Terrorist Attacks Upon the United States. The 9-11 Commission Report: Final Report of the National Commission on Terrorist Attacks Upon the United States, 26-27.

3. Congressional Research Service. *People Crossing Borders: An Analysis of US Protection Police.* (Washington, DC: US Government Printing Office, May 13, 2010), citing *A Secure Border: An Analysis of Issues Affecting the US* (Washington, DC: US Department of Justice, 1974), 1-33.

4. EPIC Mission Statement 2007. http://www.dea.gov (assessed March 2008).

5. Congressional Research Service. *Fusion Centers: Issues and Options for Congress* (Washington, DC: US Government Printing Office, January 18, 2008), 1-23.

6. Congressional Research Service. Fusion Centers: Issues and Options for Congress, 1-23.

7. Congressional Research Service. Fusion Centers: Issues and Options for Congress, 16.

8. Office of National Drug Control Policy. *US National Southwest Counternarcotics Strategy*, 26.

9. Office of National Drug Control Policy. *Anti-Drug Abuse Act of 1988 and the ONDCP Reauthorization Act of 1998.* http//www.whitehousedrugpolicy.gov (accessed April 2008).

10. Office of National Drug Control Policy. Anti-Drug Abuse Act of 1988 and the ONDCP Reauthorization Act of 1998.

11. Office of National Drug Control Policy. Anti-Drug Abuse Act of 1988 and the ONDCP Reauthorization Act of 1998.

12. Office of National Drug Control Policy. Anti-Drug Abuse Act of 1988 and the ONDCP Reauthorization Act of 1998.

13. Office of National Drug Control Policy. Anti-Drug Abuse Act of 1988 and the ONDCP Reauthorization Act of 1998.

CHAPTER 8: FIGHTING DRUGS
ALONG OUR NORTHERN BORDER

1. Chris Hawley, "At northern border, agents fight drug war on ice," http://news. yahoo. com/s/ap/20110214/ap_on_re_us/us_forgotten_border (accessed February 14, 2011).

2. US-Canada Border Drug Threat Assessment, 2007, 1-48.

3. US Department of Homeland Security, Office of Counternarcotics Enforcement. *Northern Border Counternarcotics Strategy.* (Washington, DC: Department of Homeland Security, 2008), 1-25.

4. Interview of RCMP Officials, Ontario, Canada, November 2007.

5. Interview of RCMP Officials, Ontario, Canada, November 2007.

6. Pitts, Jonathan. "Death Causes Effects of Ecstasy," *Health Guidance Report*, 2007, 1-3.

7. Pitts, Jonathan. "Death Causes Effects of Ecstasy," *Health Guidance Report*, 2007, 2-3.

8. US-Canada Border Drug Threat Assessment, 2007, 14-23.

9. US-Canada Border Drug Threat Assessment, 2007, 9-11.

10. US-Canada Border Drug Threat Assessment, 2007, 12-15.

11. US-Canada Border Drug Threat Assessment, 2007, 1-7.

12. US-Canada Border Drug Threat Assessment, 2007.

13. Public Safety Canada. *Canada's National Anti-Drug Strategy* (Ottawa, Canada: Canadian Department of Justice, 2007), 1-35.

14. Department of Homeland Security Office of Counternarcotics Enforcement Northern Border Strategy (2008); Chris Hawley, "At northern border, agents fight drug war on ice," http://news.yahoo.com/s/ap/20110214/ap_on_re_us/us_forgotten_border (accessed February 14, 2011).

15. Text: Remarks by PM Stephen Harper and US President Barack Obama, February 4, 2011, http://www.canada.com/business/Text+Remarks+Stephen+Harper+President+Barack+Obama/4227060/story.html (accessed March 19, 2011).

CHAPTER 9: FIGHTING DRUGS IN INDIAN COUNTRY

1. National Drug Intelligence Center. *National Drug Threat Assessment for Indian Country* (Washington, DC: US Government Printing Office, 2008), 1-70.

2. National Drug Intelligence Center. National Drug Threat Assessment for Indian Country, 1-21.

3. National Drug Intelligence Center. National Drug Threat Assessment for Indian Country. 27-34.

4. National Drug Intelligence Center. National Drug Threat Assessment for Indian Country, 41-44.

5. National Drug Intelligence Center. National Drug Threat Assessment for Indian Country, 51-53.

6. US-Canada Border Drug Threat Assessment, 2007, 65-67.

7. US-Canada Border Drug Threat Assessment, 2007, 68.

8. Senate Committee on Homeland Security and Governmental Affairs, *Southern Border Violence: State and Local Perspectives*, 111th Cong., 1st sess., Field Hearing, Phoenix, Arizona, April 20, 2009, 3.

9. US Department of Homeland Security. *Office of Counternarcotics Enforcement Annual Report to Congress.* (Washington, DC: US Government Printing Office, 2007), 9-10.

10. Brady McCombs, "Shadow Wolves tracking unit targets drug smugglers," *Tucson Citizen*, May 13, 2007, A2.

CHAPTER 10: THE DRUG-TERROR NEXUS

1. Christo Johnson, David Lewis and Tim Pearce, "Police seize 3 tons of marijuana," http://news.yahoo.com/s/nm/20110518/od_nm/us_sierraleone_drugs (accessed May 18, 2011).
2. United Nations. *Office of Drug Control Report for 2006* (Vienna, Austria: United Nations, 2006), 3-4.
3. United Nations. Office of Drug Control Report for 2006, 22-31.
4. Drug Enforcement Agency. *DEA Counternarcotics in Afghanistan: A DEA Perspective Brief to Capitol Hill Members* (Washington, DC: US Department of Justice, 2006) http://www.dea.gov (accessed March 10, 2010).
5. Hadari, M. A. "Afghanistan: How to Win the War on Drugs," 2009, http://www. Eurasianet.org (accessed April 20, 2011).
6. Huang, R. "Terrorism-Drugs," CDI Center for Defense Information-Security Policy and Research Organization, June 2009, http://www.CDI.org (accessed April 20, 2011).
7. President Barack Obama's Remarks to Afghanistan President Karzai, August 2009, http//www.embassyafghanisan.org (accessed April 21, 2011).
8. President Barack Obama's Remarks to Afghanistan President Karzai, August 2009, http//www.embassyafghanisan.org (accessed April 21, 2011).
9. US Department of Justice. *Inspector General Report: The Department of Justice Joint Terrorism Task Force*, (Washington, DC: US Department of Justice, June 2005), 134-137.
10. United Nations. *Office of Drug Control Report for 2007* (Vienna, Austria: United Nations, 2007), 10-13.
11. The Embassy of Afghanistan, Washington, DC, "U.S. Report Finds Declines in Opium in Afghanistan," http://www.embassyofafghanistan.org/10.24.08.html (accessed May 23, 2011).

EPILOGUE: THE BORDER CHALLENGE

1. Tim Fernholz and Jim Tankersley, "The cost of bin Laden: $3 trillion over 15 years," *National Journal*, May 6, 2011, http://www.nationaljournal.com/magazine/the-cost-of-bin-laden-3-trillion-over-15-years-20110505 (accessed May 6, 2011).
2. Tim Fernholz and Jim Tankersley, "The cost of bin Laden: $3 trillion over 15 years," *National Journal*, May 6, 2011, http://www.nationaljournal.com/magazine/the-cost-of-bin-laden-3-trillion-over-15-years-20110505 (accessed May 6, 2011).
3. 18 U.S.C. §§ 1961 *et seq.* Racketeer Influenced and Corrupt Organizations Act (RICO), Title IX of the Organized Crime Act of 1970 (P.L. 91-452).
4. Angus Reid Public Opinion, "Mexico Divided Over Capital Punishment," November 4, 2006, http://www.angus-reid.com/polls/6808/mexico_divided_over_capital_punishment (accessed June 14, 2011); Marion Lloyd, "To Live or Die in Mexico," *Global Post,* January 14, 2009, A1-A2.

5. Francis Fukuyama, "Transitions to the Rule of Law," *Journal of Democracy*, Vol. 1, No. 1, January 2010.

6. The Honorable Michael McCaul, "Bill would label drug smugglers terrorists," http://azstarnet.com/article_ 9230f15a-914b-11e0-8947-001cc4c032886.html?print=1 (accessed June 9, 2011).

7. Liz Goodwin, "Global leaders call for a major shift to decriminalize drugs," http://news.yahoo.com/s/yblog_the lookout/20110601/ts_yblog_the lookout/-global_leaders-call_for_a_major_shift_to_decriminalize_drugs (accessed June 2, 2011).

8. Veronika Oleksyn, "Experts urge reform of global drug policy," http://news.yahoo.com/ s/ap/20100628/ap_on_he_me/eu_austria_aids_policy_reform (accessed June 28, 2010).

9. Paul Stares, "Drug Legalization?: Time for a Real Debate," The Brookings Institution, Spring 1996, http://www.brookings.edu/articles/1996/spring_crime_stares.aspx?p=1 (accessed March 23, 2010).

10. T. Michael Andrews, "Mexican drug policy makes no sense," *Arizona Daily Star*, September 8, 2009.

11. Chris Hawley, "On the Border a Crisis Escalates, *USA Today*, February 23, 2009.

12. Califano, Joseph. *High Society: How Substance Abuse Ravages America and What to Do about It.* (Cambridge, MA: Public Affairs Publishing, 2007), 133-34.

13. Mike Baker, "States reassess marijuana laws after fed warnings, May 3, 2011, http://news.yahoo.com/s/ap/us_medical_marijuana_feds (accessed May 3, 2011).

14. The Brookings Institution. "Shooting Up: Counterinsurgency and the War on Drugs," Washington, DC, January 25, 2010, 5-6, http://www.brookings.edu/~/media/Files/events/2010/0125_shooting_up/20100125_shooting_up.pdf (accessed March 23, 2010).

15. The Brookings Institution. "Shooting Up: Counterinsurgency and the War on Drugs," Washington, DC, January 25, 2010, 10, http://www.brookings.edu/~/media/Files/events/ 2010/0125_shooting_up/20100125_shooting_up.pdf (accessed March 23, 2010).

16. Cristina Rayas, "US Chamber calls for integrated policy on border," http://azstarnet.com/ business/local/article_ee06d4e3-57b5-5f61-a0ff_0b6521a6b018.html (accessed June 9, 2011).

CHRONOLOGY: LEGISLATIVE MILESTONES AND POPULAR EVENTS IN CONTROLLING ILLEGAL DRUGS, 1911–2011

1. In addition to the sources cited in the endnotes below, data for this chronology are adapted from the following sources: "Thirty Years of America's Drug War: A Chronology," http://www.pbs.org/wgbh/pages/frontline/shows/drugs.cron (accessed May 10, 2010); Tom Head, "History of the War on Drugs," http://civilliberty.about.com/od/drug policy/tp/War-on-Drugs-History-Timeline.htm (accessed May 10, 2010); "United States 14 Jul 2009 Nixon war on drugs 40 years ago," July 14, 2009,

http:// www.newsahead.com/preview/2009/07/14/united-states-14-jul-2009-nixon-war-on-drugs-40-years-ago/index.php (accessed May 10, 2010); "War on Drugs," http:// en.wikipedia.org/wiki/War_on_Drugs (accessed May 10, 2010).

2. Edward Marshall, "Uncle Sam is the Worst Drug Fiend in the World," *The New York Times*, March 12, 1911, http://www.druglibrary.org/schaffer/history/e1910/worstfiend. html (accessed March 19, 2011).

3. International Narcotic Education Association, "Marihuana or Indian Hemp and Its Preparations," 1944, quoted in LaGuardia Committee Report on Marijuana, 1944, http://www.druglibrary.org/shaffer/Library/studies/lag/lagmenu.htm (accessed March 21, 2011).

4. LaGuardia Committee Report on Marijuana, 1944, http://www.druglibrary. org/shaffer/ Library/studies/lag/lagmenu.htm (accessed March 21, 2011).

5. Richard M. Nixon, "Statement on Establishing the Office for Drug Abuse Law Enforcement," January 28, 1972, http://www.presidency.ucsb.edu/ws/index. php?pid=3552#axzz1JcDJoA87 (accessed April 15, 2011).

6. Randal C. Archibold, "In Arizona Desert, Indian Trackers vs. Smugglers," http://www. nytimes.com/2007/03/07/Washington/07wolves.html (accessed March 16, 2011); "Shadow Wolves," http://en.wikipedia.org/wiki/Shadow_Wolves (last modified November 13, 2010; accessed March 16, 2011).

7. Drug Enforcement Agency, DEA History Book, 1975–1980, http://www.justice.gov/ dea/pubs/history/1975-1980.html (accessed April 15, 2011).

8. Drug Enforcement Agency, DEA History Book, 1975–1980, http://www.justice.gov/ dea/pubs/history/1975-1980.html (accessed April 15, 2011).

9. Drug Enforcement Agency, DEA History Book, 1975–1980, http://www.justice.gov/ dea/pubs/history/1975-1980.html (accessed April 15, 2011).

10. Robert H. Reid and Heidi Vogt, "DEA Agents Among 14 Americans Dead in Afghanistan," October 26, 2009, http://abcnews.go.com/International/wireStory?id= 8914054 (accessed March 16, 2010).

11. Statement by Administrator Karen P. Tandy on Two Hundred and Seven Million in Drug Money Seized in Mexico City, http://www.justice.gov/dea/pubs/pressrel/ pr032007.html (accessed March 19, 2011).

12. Theresa Cook, "US Coast Guard Makes Biggest Cocaine Bust in US History," http://abcnews.go.com/US/story?id=2970799 (accessed March 16, 2011).

13. *Kimbraugh v. United States*, 128 S.Ct 558 (2007).

14. *See, e.g.*, Andrew Selee, David Shirk and Eric Olson, "Five Myths About Mexico's Drug War," *The Washington Post*, March 28, 2010, http://www.washington-post.com/wp-dyn/content/article/2010/03/26/AR2010032602226_pf.html (accessed March 29, 2010); Mark Potter, "Border Officials Fear Growing Mexican Drug War," May 23, 2008, http://fieldnotes.msnbc.msn.com/archive/2008/05/23/1053308.aspx (accessed March 21, 2010); Mark Potter, "Mexican Drug War 'Alarming' U.S. Officials" June 25, 2008, http://worldblog.msnbc.msn.com/archive/2008/06/25/1166487. aspx (accessed March 21, 2010).

15. Interview with Gil Kerlikowske, "Q&A With the New Drug Czar," *The Wall Street Journal*, May 14, 2009, http://online.wsj.com/article/SB124233331735120871. html (accessed May 18, 2010); Office of National Drug Control Policy. *National*

Drug Control Strategy FY 2011 Budget Summary. Washington, DC, 2010, 1, http:// www.ondcp.gov/ publications/policy/11budget /fy11budget.pdf (accessed May 17, 2010).

16. Robert H. Reid and Heidi Vogt, http://abcnews.go.com/International/ wireStory?id= 8914054 (accessed March 16, 2010).

17. Drug Policy Alliance, "US Senate Unanimously Approves Bill to Reduce Crack/Power Cocaine Sentencing Disparity," http://www.drugpolicy.org/news/press-room/press release/pr031710.cfm (accessed March 16, 2011).

18. Jim Abrams, "Congress passes bill to reduce disparity in crack, powder cocaine sentencing, http://www.washingtonpost.com/wp-dyn/content/article/2010/07/28/ AR2010072802969.html?hpid=topnews (accessed March 16, 2011); National Association of Criminal Defense Lawyers, "Crack Cocaine Sentencing Reform," http:// www.nacdl.org/public.nsf/PrinterFriendly/Crack?openDocument (accessed March 16, 2011).

19. Text: Remarks by PM Stephen Harper and US President Barack Obama, February 4, 2011, http://www.canada.com/business/Text+Remarks+Stephen+Harpe r+President +Barack+Obama/4227060/story.html (accessed March 19, 2011); Chris Hawley, "At northern border, agents fight drug war on ice," http://news.yahoo.com/s/ ap/20110214/ap_on_re_us/us_forgotten_border (accessed February 14, 2011).

20. Serafin Gomez, "Who was Jaime Zapata? Hero Remembered," http://live-shots.blogs. foxnews.com/2011/02/16/who-was-jaime-zapata/ (accessed February 24, 2011).

21. Ginger Thompson and Mark Mazzetti, "US Drones Fight Mexican Drug Trade," March 15, 2011, http://www.nytimes.com/2011/03/16/world/americas/16drug.html (accessed March 18, 2011).

22. Ginger Thompson and Mark Mazzetti, http://www.nytimes.com/2011/03/16/ world/ americas/16drug.html (accessed March 18, 2011); *see also* John M. Ackerman, "Obama's Mexico Standoff," http://www.the dailybeast.com/blogs-and-stories/2011-03-02/obamas-mexico-standoff-calderon-visits-washington-amid-unrest/ full/ (accessed March 2, 2011).

23. Mike Collett-White, "Clapton guitar auction raises $2.15 million," http://www. reuters. com/article/2011/03/10/us-clapton-auction-idUSTRE7292BX20110310 (accessed March 10, 2011).

Index

Shultz, George, 87
Sinaloa Cartel, 45
smuggling. *See* drug trafficking; triple
 threat; weapons
Souder, Mark, 31
Southwest Border Initiative, 24
stability, problems of, 8, 30, 33, 82,
 84, 88, 90, 104. *See also* economic
 development
Stares, Paul, 87
State Department Bureau of
 International Narcotics and Law
 Enforcement Affairs, 15. *See also*
 Merida Initiative
State INL. *See* State Department Bureau
 of International Narcotics and Law
 Enforcement Affairs
surveillance, 11, 20, 27, 32, 34, 49, 51,
 72, 103

The Taliban, 7, 28, 80–81, 102
terrorism, 7–8, 28, 50, 56, 89–90, 101;
 definition of, 86; financing of, 30,
 80–81; responses to, 5, 17, 19, 33,
 38, 59–60, 79, 82–84. *See also* drug-
 terror nexus; The Taliban; triple
 threat
Thurmond, Strom, 17
Tijuana Cartel, 42–43, 45, 50
Tohono O' odhom Nation, 75–77, 97
transit zone, 22, 23, 26, 28, 30–31, 34, 37
treatment, 2, 24, 73, 83, 104; agencies,
 12, 14, 15; and prevention, xxiv, 15,
 18, 24, 32; budget for, 12, 32, 61,
 63, 103; debate over, 4–5, 84, 88,
 90; methadone, xxii-xxiii, 96; policy
 emphasis on, xxiii-xxiv, 11, 21,
 32, 84, 99, 102. *See also* National
 Institute on Drug Abuse
triple threat, 47–48
turf wars, 35–36, 38, 58, 62, 63, 65, 96.
 See also drug cartels, competition
 among

Twenty-first Amendment. *See*
 Prohibition, repeal of

United Nations Office of Drugs and
 Crime, 7
US Border Patrol, 25, 47, 49, 72, 77.
 See also Shadow Wolves
US Coast Guard, 11, 21, 60, 101;
 drug seizures by, 21, 27, 28–29,
 31, 102; role of, 14, 25, 35,
 37–38
US Code Title 21, 35
US Sentencing Commission. *See*
 mandatory sentencing

violence: drug, 1, 5–6, 15, 42–47,
 52, 69, 79, 80, 98, 99; spillover,
 87, 88. *See also* drug trafficking
 organizations, power of; Zetas
Volstead Act. *See* National Prohibition
 Act

Walters, John P., 17, 31, 33
war, xxi, xxiii, 27; on drugs, xxiii, 1,
 5, 6, 12, 16, 28, 38, 83, 97, 101; on
 terror, 7, 8, 83–84, 101; within a
 war, 8, 101. *See also* drug policy;
 drug wars, turf wars; stability,
 problems of
weapons, 43, 47, 51, 79; illegal,
 xix, xxvi, 33, 69, 103; of mass
 destruction, 48, 77–78
Wilson, Woodrow, 95
Woodstock Music Festival, xxii, 96
Wright, Hamilton, 94

youth: drug use, 109n7; prevention
 programs, xxii, 13, 18, 27;
 unemployment, 80

Zapata, Jaime Jorge, 103
Zedillo, Ernesto, 87
Zetas, 43–45

CPSIA information can be obtained at www.ICGtesting.com
Printed in the USA
BVOW040936091211

277876BV00005B/1/P